NOMINALISM AND REALISM
Universals and Scientific Realism
VOLUME I

Nominalism and Realism

UNIVERSALS AND SCIENTIFIC REALISM
VOLUME I

D. M. Armstrong

Challis Professor of Philosophy, University of Sydney

Cambridge University Press

CAMBRIDGE

LONDON · NEW YORK · MELBOURNE

Published by the Syndics of the Cambridge University Press
The Pitt Building, Trumpington Street, Cambridge CB2 1RP
Bentley House, 200 Euston Road, London NW1 2DB
32 East 57th Street, New York, NY 10022, USA
296 Beaconsfield Parade, Middle Park, Melbourne 3206, Australia

First published 1978

Printed in Great Britain by
Cox & Wyman Ltd,
London, Fakenham and Reading

Library of Congress Cataloguing in Publication Data Revisea

Armstrong, David Malet.
Universals and scientific realism.

Includes bibliographies and indexes.
CONTENTS: v. 1. Nominalism and realism.
– v. 2. A theory of universals.
1. Universals (Philosophy) 2. Realism.
3. Nominalism. I. Title.
B105. U5A75   111   77–80824

ISBN 0 521 21741 5

THESE VOLUMES ARE DEDICATED
TO THE MEMORY OF
PROFESSOR JOHN ANDERSON

ACKNOWLEDGMENTS

The following persons have read the whole or part of various drafts of *Universals and Scientific Realism*, and have helped me greatly with comments, criticism and encouragement: Keith Campbell, Lauchlan Chipman, Len Goddard, Frank Jackson, Bruce Langtry, Tom Rose, Jack Smart, Michael Tooley, Gail Tulloch and the anonymous referees for the Cambridge University Press. I have also profited greatly from seminars on the topic of universals which I have given for a number of years at Sydney University and also, during 1976, at Latrobe and Melbourne Universities. I am greatly indebted to Pat Trifonoff and Jackie Walter for typing successive drafts.

Despite the political upheavals in our universities in recent years, the Australian philosophical community has remained a good one to work in.

Sydney University   D.M.A.

May 1977

Contents

Volume II: A Theory of Universals
The argument of Volume I

PART FOUR PREDICATES AND UNIVERSALS

PART SEVEN HIGHER-ORDER UNIVERSALS

Introduction

It is argued in this work, first, that there are universals, both monadic and polyadic, that is, properties and relations, which exist independently of the classifying mind. Realism is thus accepted, Nominalism rejected. Second, it is argued that no monadic universal is found except as a property of some particular, and no polyadic universal except as a relation holding between particulars. Transcendent or Platonic Realism is thus rejected. Third, it is argued that what universals there are is not to be determined simply by considering what predicates can be applied to particulars. Instead, it is the task of total science, conceived of as total enquiry, to determine what universals there are. The view defended is therefore a *scientific* Realism about universals. It might also be called *a posteriori* Realism. The working out of a scientific Realism about universals is intended to be the special contribution of these volumes.

Contemporary philosophy recognizes two main lines of argument for the existence of objective universals. The first is, or is a descendant of, Plato's One over Many argument. Its premiss is that many different particulars can all have what appears to be the same nature. In the terms used by C. S. Peirce, different *tokens* may all be of the same *type*. The conclusion of the argument is simply that in general this appearance cannot be explained away, but must be accepted. There is such a thing as identity of nature.

I take this argument to be sound. But the argument is sometimes presented as an argument from general words. It is asked how a general term can be applied to an indefinite multiplicity of particulars. It is answered that these particulars must be identical in some respect. There are two disadvantages in presenting the argument in this linguistic fashion. First, it obscures the fact that the same term may apply in virtue of different natures of the different particulars. As a result, where Realism is embraced, it is likely to be *a priori* rather than scientific Realism. Second, presenting the argument linguistically encourages confusion with an unsound argument to universals from *meaning*.

This second argument moves from the existence of meaningful general words to the existence of universals which are the meanings of those words. Universals are postulated as the second term of the meaning relation. The argument from ideal cases, such as Plato's perfect circle, is perhaps a special case of this semantic argument to universals.

I regard this second line of argument as completely unsound. Furthermore, I believe that the identification of universals with meanings (connotations, intensions), which this argument presupposes, has been a disaster for the theory of universals. A thoroughgoing separation of the theory of universals from the theory of the semantics of general terms is in fact required. Only if we first develop a satisfactory theory of universals can we expect to develop fruitfully the further topic of the semantics of general terms. Philosophers have all too often tried to proceed in the opposite way.

In this first volume, *Nominalism and Realism*, I criticize at length and reject various versions of Nominalism, together with Platonic Realism. I also examine and reject the view that properties and relations are as particular as the objects which have properties and relations. I conclude that we must admit objective universals which, however, cannot exist independently of particulars. I go on to examine the notion of a particular and reject the view that we can give an account of particulars as "bundles of universals". The conclusion drawn is that particularity and universality, irreducible to each other, are both involved in all existence. I end the first book by sketching a world-hypothesis which admits nothing but particulars having (universal) properties and relations.

The position reached at that point, though contested by many, is, at least in general outline, familiar enough. But in the second volume a detailed attempt is made to work out a theory of universals which is based upon natural science. In making this attempt, I enter relatively unexplored territory. For with the exception of a suggestive paper by Hilary Putnam (1970a) contemporary philosophers, at least, have largely ignored the possibility of developing a theory of objective universals, where the particular universals admitted are determined on the basis of scientific rather than semantic considerations. It might perhaps be argued that Plato in his later works, Aristotle and the Scholastic Realists were ahead of contemporary philosophy in this matter, although handicapped by the relative backwardness of the science and the scientific methodology of their day.

My contention is that, by accepting this *a posteriori* Realism, the theory of universals, arguably the central problem of ontology, can be placed on a securer and more intelligible foundation than anything previously available. In particular, such a doctrine makes possible the reconciliation of an empiricist epistemology, which I wish to retain, with ontological realism about universals.

Not all particulars are first-order particulars. Universals themselves fall under universals. That is to say, universals have certain properties and stand in certain relations to each other. In the final part of the second book an attempt is made to work out a theory of higher-order universals, but, again, one which is compatible with an empiricist epistemology. Of quite particular importance is the topic of *relations* between universals. For this topic may hold the key to an account of the nature of causation and of nomic necessity. By this means, it may prove possible to answer Hume without sacrificing Empiricism.

Finally, a word on the phrase "*a posteriori* Realism". The phrase may suggest that the theory advanced in this work is supposed to be supported by *a posteriori* reasonings of the sort with which natural science has made us familiar. This is far from being the case. The reasoning will have the characteristically *a priori* flavour which philosophical reasonings, especially when they concern first philosophy, seem inevitably, if distressingly, to have. What is maintained is the proposition that what universals there are is to be determined *a posteriori*. The status of this proposition is, however, a further question. It may have to be established, if it can be established, by *a priori* or relatively *a priori* reasoning.

PART ONE
PRELIMINARIES

I

Predicates

I *Predicates as linguistic expressions*

Before considering the topic of universals directly, it will be necessary to say something about the notion of a *predicate*.

Although the word "predicate" is a term of art, it is one which is both enriched and encumbered by a long tradition of philosophical discussion in which it has been both used and mentioned. As a result, an exact definition is a hazardous business. Fortunately, however, our purposes do not require such a definition. It will be sufficient simply to indicate in an informal way what is to be understood by the term.

Consider, then, the contemporary logician's dummy sentence "Fa" which is used in place of such sentences as "This is circular" or "Socrates is a man". Any linguistic expression for which the "F" is a suitable dummy is a one-place predicate. Again, in the logician's dummy sentence "Rab", used in place of such sentences as "This is to the left of that" and "John loves Jane", any linguistic expression for which "R" is a suitable dummy is a two-place predicate. Of course, logicians dispute about just how large a class of linguistic expressions "F" and "R" are suitable dummies for. For our purposes here it will be convenient to be extremely tolerant about admitting linguistic expressions into the class. Since it is a central contention of this work that there are indefinitely many predicates to which no universals correspond, such tolerance will have no ontological consequences. For instance, I should admit "exists" as a predicate although denying that existence is a property (or relation).

This informal way of explaining the notion of a predicate also enables an informal explanation to be given of a subject term. In the dummy sentences "Fa" and "Rab" any linguistic expression for which "a" or "b" is a suitable dummy is a subject term. Once again, I wish to be very tolerant about what expressions are admitted into the class.

Given a sentence having the form "Fa", and given that the thing *a* actually exists, we can say that "F" is *predicated of a*. Predicating "F" of *a* may yield a false proposition. It may not be the case that *a* is F. But if and only if this predication yields a true proposition, then "F" may be said to *apply to a*. Instead of saying that "F" applies to *a*, many philosophers speak of "F" being *true of a*. I prefer to avoid the phrase "true of" in this context. My reasons will emerge shortly.

But exactly what portions of sentences should we account predicates? There appear to be three alternatives. The first is to account as predicates words such as "circular" and phrases such as "to the left of". The second is to expand these expressions into the phrases "is circular" and "is to the left of". The third is to identify predicates with sentence-frames such as "——— is circular" and "——— is to the left of ———".

Strawson (1974, pp. 37–8) gives a strong argument for identifying predicates with sentence-frames. He points out that it is part of the *meaning* of different predicates that they are one- or two- or three- or . . . -place predicates. For example, if somebody thought that "to the left of" could be predicated of a single thing, then he would have failed to understand what the expression means. Predicates "accept" just so many subject terms. Subject terms, by comparison, are not restricted in this way. They accept predicates with any number of subject-positions. Justice is done to this feature of predicates if they are identified with "gappy" sentences, that is, with sentence-frames.

It may be remarked in passing that there is a common ontological view that particulars are independent existences but that their properties and relations are dependent entities. I believe this view to be at best thoroughly misleading. Particularity and universality, it will be argued, are aspects of all reality and of equal rank. But does not the relative independence of subject terms in a sentence, and the relative dependence of predicates, encourage philosophers to draw corresponding conclusions about particulars and universals? If so, we may have uncovered here one, though certainly only one, of the hidden roots of Nominalism.

But a reservation must be made about the identification of

predicates with sentence-frames. There is no reason why the copula "is" should be accounted part of the predicate. I would prefer to represent the predicates as "——— [is] circular" or "——— [is] to the left of ———". Copulation of subject term(s) with a predicate is best represented as a filling in of the blank(s). It does not fall within the predicate. (The logician's "Fa" is thus a more satisfactory symbolism.) The desire to force the copula within the predicate seems again to be connected with the attempt to make particulars independent and universals dependent beings.

We must, of course, remember the ambiguity of "is". It may have the force of "is identical with". Then the phrase "identical with" is part of a predicate. Again, "is" may have the force of "is now" and once again the word "now" is part of the predicate and/or part of the subject term. But where "is" is simply the copula, it should be excluded both from the predicate and the subject term.

Strictly, then, predicates should be identified with certain copula-purged sentence-frames. But, having argued this, it will do no harm to the purposes of this work, and will make for orthographic simplicity, if we once again contract the representation of predicates to such expressions as "circular" and "to the left of". The gaps can be understood, not represented.

Gaps or no gaps, copula or no copula, predicates in this work are taken to be linguistic expressions. In taking predicates to be linguistic expressions, and so parts of sentences, I am following the usage of contemporary and also mediaeval philosophers (for the latter see Kretzmann, 1970, p. 768). But there is another tradition which goes back to the Stoics and which was dominant between the mediaeval and strictly contemporary period. This tradition took predicates not to be parts of sentences, but rather *parts of propositions*.

The two traditions would fail to be distinct if sentences were identical with propositions. However, this identification cannot be made. We can, for instance, ask of a sentence what language it is a sentence of. Is it an English or a French sentence? Now the class of English sentences has few, if any, members which are also members of the class of French sentences. But there are many pairs of English and French sentences which "express the same proposition". So it is not the case that sentence = proposition. The logical relations of sentences and propositions may be very close. At any rate, the argument just given does not rule out close relation. But the relation is not that of identity. So the tradition which makes predicates parts of sentences is certainly a different tradition from that which makes predicates parts of propositions.[1]

Light can be cast upon the ambiguity of the term "predicate" by noticing similar ambiguities in the meaning of some other terms. Consider the word "belief". It may mean a mental existent, something in somebody's mind. In this sense of the word, beliefs are acquired, retained and lost. But it may also mean what is believed, the *content* of the belief in the first sense, a certain proposition. (We believe propositions, not sentences.) Beliefs in this second sense cannot be acquired or lost. What is believed is not a mental existent at all, although, of course, it is only spoken of as a belief in virtue of the fact that it is the "content" of something mental. In the first sense of the word "belief" we can draw a distinction between belief-token and belief-type. If two people both believe that the earth is flat, then there are two belief-tokens but only one belief-type. But if the word "belief" means "what is believed", *viz.* the proposition that the earth is flat, then it makes no sense to speak of different tokens of the same proposition.

These two senses of the word "belief" are exactly parallel to the two traditions among philosophers of use of the word "predicate". Predicates may be linguistic expressions or they may be what is predicated by the linguistic expressions. If by "predicate" we mean a linguistic entity, then we can distinguish between predicate-types and predicate-tokens. Suppose that two speakers both utter sentences which contain the predicate "F". They bring into existence two distinct tokens of the same predicate-type. But if by "predicate" is meant part of a proposition, then there is no room to distinguish different tokens of the same type. There is just the predicate F.

Other terms exhibit the same sort of ambiguity. Some are mental terms, such as "desire". Others, like the term "predicate", are semantic terms. The term "statement", for instance, may refer to speech-acts of stating. The distinction between type and token then applies. But it may refer to what is stated (the proposition stated) and then no such distinction can be drawn.

[1] It is very unfortunate that quotation-marks are conventionally used by philosophers to refer both to sentences and to propositions. This may help to obscure the fact that they are not identical, although I do not know whether the convention is more cause or effect of the confusion. In this work, quotation-marks around a sentence always form the name of the *sentence*, usually the sentence-type, never the proposition. For the best account that I know of the way in which quotation-marks are used to form the name of linguistic expressions see Barnett, 1974.

It is to be noted further that the ambiguity of words like "belief" and "statement" is, on the whole, a convenient ambiguity in ordinary discourse. It is often useful for a speaker to be able to pass freely back and forth between belief-state and belief-content, between the stating and what is stated, without having to note the passage explicitly. The hearer usually disambiguates the word without any difficulty, without even realizing what he is doing.

Our purposes, however, require that we take explicit note of the ambiguity. I propose therefore to adopt the contemporary usage and reserve the term "predicate" when used by itself without a qualifier for *certain linguistic expressions*. Where there is occasion to speak of predicates in the other sense I will speak explicitly of the predicates of propositions, or of propositional predicates.

One reason I have for following the contemporary usage is that I do not really believe that there are such things as propositions. And if there are no propositions, there are no parts of propositions and so there are no predicates in the second sense of "predicate". In saying that there are no such things as propositions and predicates of propositions I am not denying that the term "proposition" and the phrase "predicate of a proposition" frequently occur in sentences which themselves "express true propositions". Indeed, these terms, or their equivalents, seem to be in practice indispensable. But I do not think that there are entities called propositions which have parts. The following is a parallel. There is no such thing as the average man. Nevertheless, the phrase "the average man" occurs in sentences which express truths. It is, indeed, an indispensable phrase in certain contexts. I believe that the same is true of "proposition" and "predicate of a proposition". However, it still seems proper to reserve the term "predicate" for something which does actually exist: *viz*. certain sorts of expression. (For some further discussion of propositions, see Armstrong, 1973, ch. 4.)

If a sentence expresses a certain proposition, then it is natural, and I think correct, to identify the proposition with the *meaning* of that sentence. (If there are propositions to which there correspond no sentences, then these propositions will be *possible meanings*.) Hence, if propositions do not exist, then meanings of sentences do not exist either. Talk about such meanings, however, may still be just as legitimate as talk about the average man, and I believe that it is in fact indispensable in semantics.

If propositions are the meanings of sentences, then propositional predicates would appear to be the meanings of (linguistic) predicates. This is of great importance for the theory of universals. Realists about universals, at any rate, have often identified universals with propositional predicates, or some suitable sub-set of propositional predicates. The theory of universals is then brought into very close connection with the theory of meaning. The denial that there are such things as meanings can then be used as a premiss in an argument to show that Realism is false and that there are no universals.

In this work, however, it will be denied that universals (properties and relations) can be identified with propositional predicates. This will represent an emancipation of the theory of universals from the theory of semantics.

Before turning it to the question of identity-conditions for predicates, it should be noticed that in their ordinary use the expressions "true" and "false" are applied to propositions rather than sentences. We do not say that the sentence "Socrates is wise" is true (or false). Rather, we say that what this sentence is used to assert, the proposition that Socrates is wise, is true (or false). This is why I am unwilling to say that the predicate "wise" is *true of* Socrates, and instead prefer to speak of it as *applying to* Socrates. The terms "proposition", "meaning", "true" and "false" all belong at the same level of discourse.

II *Identity-conditions for predicates*

What are the identity-conditions for predicates? When do we have the same or different predicates? We are not here concerned with identity-conditions for predicate-tokens, which will be much the same as those for many other physical phenomena, but with identity-conditions for predicate-types. Or, to put the matter perhaps more positively, we are concerned with the conditions under which different predicate-tokens are accounted different instances of the identical predicate-type.

It is not clear that there is a true answer to be found to this question. Rather, it is a matter of choosing those identity-conditions which are most suitable for the theoretical task in hand. For some purposes the identity-conditions are given by phonetic and/or orthographic criteria. Two tokens of the predicate "bank" would then be tokens of the same predicate-type despite the fact that, in the sentences in which they occurred, they had different meanings. Similarly a token of the predicate "ophthalmologist" would be a token of a different predicate-type from a token of the predicate "eye-doctor" despite the fact that the two tokens had the same meaning.

For our purposes, however, phonetic or orthographic criteria of identity would be most inconvenient. Although we have distinguished predicates, which are linguistic entities, from "propositional predicates", which are "parts" of propositions, it is obviously convenient to correlate the two sorts of predicates in some simple way. This would be achieved if linguistic predicate-tokens were said to be of the same type if and only if they expressed the very same propositional predicate. But propositional predicates are meanings. Hence it is convenient to say that different predicate-tokens are of the same type if and only if they are synonymous. Predicates (as opposed to propositional predicates) are linguistic entities, but the criterion for identity of their type is *semantic*.[1]

It is useful, however, to retain a way of referring to predicates where their identity-conditions remain phonetic and/or orthographic. Following a suggestion made by Frank Jackson I will from this point on use double quotation-marks for predicates whose type identity-conditions are phonetic–orthographic, and single quotation-marks for predicates whose type identity-conditions are semantic.

Thus:

"opthalmologist"	=	"OPTHALMOLOGIST"
"bank"	=	"bank" (whatever the meaning)
"opthalmologist"	≠	"eye-doctor"
"red"	≠	"rouge"

but

'opthalmologist'	=	'eye-doctor'
'red'	=	'rouge'

although

'human'	≠	'featherless biped'.

(The '=' sign is here intended only to assert identity of predicate type.)

It is presumably no objection to the notion of synonymy that while some predicates are clearly synonymous and others are clearly

---

[1] The distinction between phonetic–orthographic and semantic criteria of identity seems to correspond to Abelard's distinction between *vox* and *sermo*.

non-synonymous, borderline cases can be found where it is not clear what the situation is and in which, perhaps, any decision must be arbitrary. For in this respect the concept of synonymy resembles most, perhaps all, other empirical concepts.

W. V. Quine has placed the notion of synonymy under a cloud by declaring it to be an incoherent concept. I shall therefore say briefly why I reject Quine's strictures.

First, unlike such concepts as analyticity or logical necessity, synonymy is an untechnical concept freely employed in ordinary thought and discourse. The actual word "synonymy" is a technical one. But the notion of sameness (and difference) of meaning is one which we constantly employ and appeal to. The notion is applied to a body of material, *viz.* linguistic expressions, which everybody agrees to exist; and there is very widespread non-collusive agreement as to what expressions are synonymous and what are not. Indeed, the notion has such deep roots in our ordinary talk and thought about linguistic matters that we do not know how to dispense with it in that talk and thought. Now a concept which has these characteristics has an extremely strong claim to be a coherent concept.

But it is not merely the case that the notions of sameness and difference of meaning are indispensable in the course of our ordinary, untheoretical, talk and reflection about linguistic matters. The notions are also indispensable to the science of linguistics as it is at present conceived and practised, a science which is making far greater progress now than at any other time in its history. In the recent past, under the influence of Behaviourist thinking, linguists tried to dispense with the 'mentalistic' notion of meaning. But their attempt is generally held to have failed. Consider the notions of *paraphrase* and *ambiguity*. These notions are essential tools of Chomskian and post-Chomskian linguistics. Their theoretical usefulness and fruitfulness is not in doubt. Yet a paraphrase of a sentence is another sentence which means the same as the original sentence. An ambiguous sentence or phrase is a sentence or phrase which can mean different things.

So both commonsense and science use, and seemingly cannot dispense with, the notion of synonymy. All that can be said against the notion is the undeniable fact that it has proved exceedingly difficult to give any satisfactory philosophical account or logical analysis of synonymy. But this fact I take to be simply a tribute to the great difficulty of the task. It is, after all, notorious how difficult it can be to pass from a practically satisfactory but unselfconscious grasp of some notion which is central in our thought to an explicit account of the logical structure of that notion. It would not be surprising if this held in the case of synonymy.

So it is granted that the notion of synonymy is philosophically opaque, but it is urged that this is no reason for jettisoning it. It may still be, and I believe is, the most satisfactory criterion to use for the type identity of tokens of predicates.

Having made these preliminary remarks about predicates we can embark on the direct examination of the Problem of Universals, beginning with a consideration of Nominalism.

PART TWO

THEORIES OF UNIVERSALS

... that old man of the sea, nominalism, which has ridden so much modern empiricism.
Donald Williams (1966, p. 223)

2

Predicate Nominalism

1 *Nominalism versus Realism*

There is one sense in which everybody agrees that particulars have properties and stand in relations to other particulars. The piece of paper before me is a particular. It is white, so it has a property. It rests upon a table, so it is related to another particular. Such gross facts are not, or should not be, in dispute between Nominalists and Realists.

G. E. Moore never tired of emphasizing that in the case of many of the great metaphysical disputes the gross facts are not in dispute. What is in dispute, he contended, is the account or analysis to be given of the gross facts. This appears to be the situation in the dispute between Nominalism and Realism. Both can agree that the paper is white and rests upon a table. It is an adequacy-condition of their analyses that such statements come out true. But the analyses themselves are utterly different.

We start with a basic agreement, then: that in some minimal or pre-analytic sense there are things having certain properties and standing in certain relations. But, as Plato was the first to point out, this situation is a profoundly puzzling one, at least for philosophers. The same property can belong to different things. The same relation can relate different things. Apparently, there can be something identical in things which are not identical. Things are one at the same time as they are many. How is this possible? Nominalists and Realists react to the puzzle in different ways.

Nominalists deny that there is any genuine or objective identity in things which are not identical. Realists, on the other hand, hold that the apparent situation is the real situation. There genuinely is, or can be, something identical in things which are not identical. Besides particulars, there are universals.

The fundamental contention of Nominalism is that *all things that exist are only particulars*. The Realist need not deny that all things that exist are particulars, but he must at least deny that there are *only* particulars. The mirror-image of Nominalism is not Realism but what might be called the "Universalist" doctrine that *nothing but universals exist*. Such "Universalism" faces an opposite but equal problem to Nominalism: that of giving an account of the apparent existence of particulars. Attempts have been made to solve the problem by arguing that particulars are nothing but bundles of universals (*properties*, specifically).

For the present, however, we are concerned with the problems of the Nominalist. How is he to account for the apparent (if usually partial) identity of numerically different particulars? How can two different things both be white or both be on a table? It is natural for the Nominalist to pose his problem in linguistic terms. Locke summed the matter up with admirable and quite unusual succinctness when he said:

> since all things that exist are only particulars how come we by general terms ...?

> (*Essay*, Bk. III, ch. 3 §10)

However, although all Nominalists agree that all things that exist are only particulars, they by no means agree about the way that the problem of apparent identity of nature is to be solved. I classify their attempted solutions under five heads which I call Predicate Nominalism, Concept Nominalism, Class Nominalism, Mereological Nominalism and Resemblance Nominalism. In the next section I explain these five positions (the latter four, only briefly). The rest of the chapter will then be devoted to criticizing Predicate Nominalism.

II *Varieties of Nominalism*

Predicate Nominalism. Some predicates, such as 'identical with the planet Venus' or, perhaps, 'the wisest of men' apply to one and only one thing. But other predicates, such as 'circular' and 'man' apply to indefinitely, perhaps infinitely, many things. These latter are Locke's "general terms". The question arises "In virtue of what do these general terms apply to the things which they apply to?" The answer of Predicate Nominalism is "In virtue of nothing". The fundamental fact in this situation, which cannot be further explained, is that the predicates do apply.

Restricting ourselves for simplicity to one-place predicates, we can say that Predicate Nominalists give the following analysis:

> a has the property, F, if and only if
> a falls under the predicate 'F'.

Falling under, of course, is simply the converse of *applying to*.[1] This equivalence might be accepted by other philosophers besides Predicate Nominalists. For the Predicate Nominalist, however, the right-hand side must be taken to be a logical analysis, a *reductive* analysis, of the left-hand side. For the Predicate Nominalist the *Realists'* properties – objective properties – are nothing but a shadow cast upon particulars by predicates. Imagine the system of predicates as a grille, and the particulars which they apply to as a surface. If the grille casts a shadow upon the surface, then there may *appear* to be a physical grille actually etched upon the surface.

It follows that, although the property is conventionally symbolized as F and the predicate as 'F', from the point of view of the Predicate Nominalist the greater orthographic complexity of the predicate symbol is misleading. For it is the predicate which is the unanalysed primitive in his analysis and the property which is defined by means of the predicate.

The relation of *applying to* which holds between predicate and particular may also be said to be the relation of *being true of*. But I have explained at the end of ch. 1 § 1 why I think it is misleading to say that predicates, which are linguistic expressions, are "true of" objects.

In old-fashioned representations of Predicate Nominalism it is sometimes said that the predicate 'F' is a *name*. It differs from an expression such as '*a*' in being a "common" name. However there seems to be no reason for, and many reasons against, the Predicate Nominalist adopting a "two-name" theory of predication. It is better to see the semantic relation between 'F' and *a* as a different

---

[1] When I wish to refer to a putative property or relation I will italicize the corresponding expression.

sort of relation from that holding between 'a' and *a*, or, at least, not to prejudge any question about the differences or similarities between the two relations.

It should be noted that the term "Nominalism" is sometimes restricted to the position which I call *Predicate* Nominalism. And, indeed, this would be the most appropriate nomenclature. Nominalism in the broad sense of the term, the doctrine that all things that exist are only particulars, would better be called "Particularism". Nor is "Realism" a particularly happy term for the opponents of Nominalism. But the tradition of calling the two main camps in the dispute about universals "Nominalists" and "Realists" is so deeply entrenched that I do not think it can be overthrown. Unable to beat it, I join it. In any case, the term "Particularism" can usefully be reserved for the doctrine that properties and relations, though objective, are particulars not universals (see ch. 8).

Are there any Predicate Nominalists? Is the doctrine really just a straw man or ideal case, approached, but never reached, by actual Nominalists? Even if this were true, criticism of Predicate Nominalism would have its value. But I do not think it is true. We may, for instance, cite John Searle (1969):

> Insofar as the nominalist is claiming that the existence of particulars depends on facts in the world and the existence of universals merely on the meaning of words, he is quite correct. But he lapses into confusion and needless error if his discovery leads him to deny such trivially true things as that there is such a property as the property of being red and that centaurhood exists. For to assert these need commit one to no more than that certain predicates have a meaning. (p. 105)

Again:

> to put it briefly, universals are parasitic upon predicate expressions... (p. 120)

Concept Nominalism. The Concept Nominalist calls upon concepts, conceived as mental entities, to do the job for which the Predicate Nominalist employs predicates. For him:

> a has the property, F, if and only if
> a falls under the concept *F*.

This relation of *falling under* is not the same relation as that which holds between *a* and 'F', but it is systematically correlated with the latter relation. Once we have criticized Predicate Nominalism we shall find that the minor differences in doctrine created by the switch from predicates to concepts require no very extensive independent examination.

Class Nominalism. For the Class Nominalist:

> a has the property, F, if and only if
> a is a member of the class of Fs.

I have not found an author who explicitly expounds and defends Class Nominalism. Rather, Class Nominalism is a pervasive tendency or occasional assumption among those philosophers who are Nominalist in sympathy, particularly if they are logicians. For modern logic has an extensional or class bias.

Quine would consider the phrase "Class Nominalism" to be self-contradictory. But this is because of his historically eccentric use of the term "Nominalism". For Quine, "Nominalism" has been abandoned, and "Platonism" embraced, if "abstract entities" are introduced. Although, as far as I know, he nowhere tell us what he means by an abstract entity, he does account classes as abstract entities. I shall be pointing out in ch. 4 that classes of particulars are themselves particulars. If this is correct, and if we accept the traditional use of the term "Nominalism", what I call Class Nominalism is a form of Nominalism.

Mereological Nominalism. For this variant of Class Nominalism:

> a has the property, F, if and only if
> a is a part of the aggregate
> (heap) of the Fs.

It will be briefly discussed in the chapter on Class Nominalism.

Resemblance Nominalism. Resemblance Nominalism is the most carefully articulated form of Nominalism, and both Carnap (1967) and Price (1953) have presented fully worked-out Resemblance Nominalisms. According to this view:

> a has the property, F, if and only if
> a suitably resembles a paradigm case
> (or paradigm cases) of an F.

'Suitable resemblance' here is simply a brief dummy for the much more elaborate account, somewhat different in different versions, which is given by Resemblance Nominalists.

This brief account of Concept, Class, Mereological and Resemblance Nominalism is given here simply to illuminate Predicate Nominalism a little further by comparison and contrast. It will be noticed that all five analyses have a common form. In each case, *a*'s having a certain property is analysed as a matter of *a*'s having some relation, R, to an entity, ø, for various R and ø. The analyses may therefore be said to be *Relational* theories of universals. *Platonic* Realism is also a Relational theory, although it involves an R and a ø of a more mysterious sort. We shall see that the difficulties faced by all Relational theories are very similar.

I do not claim that the five varieties just explained exhaust the varieties of Nominalism. For instance, M. J. Cresswell (1975) has given an ingenious (if to me not entirely convincing) reconstruction of Aristotle's theory of universals:

> which is not ontologically committed to the existence of anything other than particulars. (p. 241)

This "Aristotelian Nominalism" is more complex than any of the analyses just outlined. But I do claim that the criticisms of Nominalisms to be developed in the following chapters can be used to refute any form of Nominalism, including Cresswell's Aristotle.

It may be noticed also that in practice the different types of Nominalism are not very sharply cut off from each other. There is always a tendency for proponents of one variety, particularly under pressure, to pass to another analysis in the course of exposition or argument. The reason for this, I suppose, is that the Nominalist's real attachment is to the doctrine that whatever exists is only a particular. Provided this doctrine is secure, the particular solution he adopts in order to solve the problem of apparent identity of nature or kind is a matter of secondary concern to the Nominalist.

Besides the five versions of Nominalism already outlined, we should perhaps include a sixth: Ostrich or Cloak-and-dagger Nominalism. I have in mind those philosophers who refuse to countenance universals but who at the same time see no need for any reductive analyses of the sorts just outlined. There are no universals but the proposition that *a* is F is perfectly all right as it is. Quine's refusal to take predicates with any ontological seriousness seems to make him a Nominalist of this kind.

What such a Nominalist is doing is simply refusing to give any account of the type/token distinction, and, in particular, any account of types. But, like anybody else, such a Nominalist will make continual *use* of the distinction. *Prima facie*, it is incompatible with Nominalism. He therefore owes us an account of the distinction. It is a compulsory question in the examination paper.

If more direct argument against such a Nominalist is asked for, I appeal to the considerations advanced by Arthur Pap and refined by Frank Jackson. These considerations will be recapitulated in ch. 6. Another argument is given in ch. 5 § III.

III *Can predicates determine properties?*

Beginning with this section, I consider various objections to Predicate Nominalism. I believe that they are all conclusive. §v considers and rejects a reformulation of Predicate Nominalism in terms of the applicability of *possible* predicates.

According to Predicate Nominalism, an object's possession of (say) the property, *being white*, is completely determined by the fact that the predicate 'white' applies to this object. But now let us make a thought-experiment. Let us imagine that the predicate 'white' does not exist. Is it not obvious that the object might still be white? If so, its whiteness is *not* constituted by the object's relation to the predicate 'white'.

The argument is not apodeictic. It depends upon inspection. But such inspection reveals that the applicability of 'white' depends upon the whiteness of the object, not the whiteness of the object upon the applicability of 'white'.

It is very important not to overestimate how much this argument establishes, even if it is sound. It does not establish that the predicate 'white' applies to the object in virtue of the objective property of *whiteness*. We shall see at a much later point (in the second volume) that there is good reason to think that, even if Realism is true, there is no such objective property as *whiteness*. Indeed, the attempt to use this argument to move straight from predicates to properties has, in my judgment, been a factor in discrediting Realism. Empiricist philosophers, in particular, have felt that the facts from which the argument starts are insufficiently weighty to justify so sweeping a conclusion. We start from the correct application of a predicate and in a moment we are forced to postulate a universal. It is far too sudden!

I think that the Empiricist suspicion is perfectly justified here. All that the argument shows is that there must be something about the particular, besides the fact that it is a particular, to explain why the predicate 'white' applies to it. Many different accounts of this something may still be possible. It is not even necessary that the same account be given in the case of every applicable predicate. The argument shows no more than it shows: that the Predicate Nominalist's account of what it is for something to be white is inadequate.

It may be suggested that the Predicate Nominalist's analysis is not so much inadequate as incomplete. Perhaps the doctrine of predicates requires only to be supplemented by some account of what it is about different particulars which makes different predicates applicable to them. But although this suggestion is plausible enough when put forward in an abstract fashion, it seems not to be susceptible of fruitful development. For instance, the classical method of trying to overcome the difficulties of Predicate Nominalism is to appeal to the *resemblance* which particulars falling under the same predicate have to each other: "the similitudes in things" as Locke put it. But once a Resemblance analysis is worked out in any detail, then the account of what it is for a thing to have a property can best proceed in terms of resemblances alone. There are no advantages in appealing to predicates also. Predicate Nominalism simply turns into Resemblance Nominalism.

Again, it may be suggested that the predicates which apply to objects are not applied to them arbitrarily, but apply in virtue of the way in which the objects act upon our sense-organs. Difference of predicate corresponds to difference of such action, a suggestion which is perhaps in the spirit of Quine. But the different way in which objects act upon us is, of course, a different *sort* of way. Two points then arise. First, will not this different sort of action depend upon the different nature of the things which act? And what account will the Predicate Nominalist give of this difference of nature? Second, what is it for us to be affected in different *sorts* of way? These problems are versions of the original problem about properties which the Predicate Nominalist analysis was intended to solve.

IV *Predicate Nominalism and two infinite regresses*[1]

Before embarking upon the argument of this section, it will be helpful to recall what was said at the beginning of this chapter.

[1] This section, together with the discussion of infinite regress arguments in chs. 3, 4, 5 and 7 is based upon Armstrong (1974).

What was pointed out there in effect was that, in the dispute between Realism and Nominalism, the onus of proof lies with the latter. Ordinary thought and discourse recognizes identity both of particulars and of property, sort or kind. Indeed, without the distinction between sameness of thing and sameness of property or kind, thought and discourse would be impossible. The terms "token" and "type" are terms of art, but the distinction which they mark is admitted by everybody. All that the Nominalist can hope to do is to give a reductive analysis or account of what it is for something to have a property or to be of a certain kind or sort: a reductive analysis or account of types.

If, then, in the course of an attempted Nominalist analysis it should happen that covert appeal is made to the notion of property, kind or type, the analysis has failed to achieve its purpose. The failure does not prove the truth of Realism, but it does show that that particular Nominalist analysis has failed in its purpose.

Various of the following arguments, in particular the infinite regress arguments against the varieties of Nominalism, depend upon this point. They aim to show that the Nominalist gives a reductive account of certain types only at the cost of reinstating further types, which is no advance. I now attempt to show this for the case of *Predicate* Nominalism.

Given a class, such as the class of white things, the Predicate Nominalist seeks to give an account of its unity by saying that each member of this class has the same relation (the relation of *falling under*) to the same predicate: the predicate 'white'. But the two samenesses involved here are not samenesses of a particular, rather they are samenesses of sort, kind or type. Each white thing has the same sort of relation to the predicate 'white'. Nor do they have this type of relation to just one token of the predicate. They have this type of relation to any token of the predicate-type 'white'.

Types, however, are the very phenomenon to be reduced. So the Predicate Nominalist has covertly appealed to types in the course of developing a theory which claims to give a reductive analysis of all types. It is clear that, if he is to be consistent, those types which appear on the right-hand side of his analyses must themselves be analysed in Predicate Nominalist style. But such analysis requires appeal to types, and so *ad infinitum*. The theory is involved in an infinite regress. I shall argue that the regress is vicious.

We may distinguish between the *Object* regress, which involves the predicate, and the *Relation* regress, which involves the relation between object and predicate. This terminology will be found to be of service not only in the examination of Predicate Nominalism, but in the case of all *Relational* analyses of what it is for a particular to have a property or for two or more particulars to be related in a certain sort of way.

The Object regress arises because the Predicate Nominalist must be understood to mean that the whiteness of white objects is constituted by their special relationship to tokens of the predicate-*type* 'white'. But what account can he give of this type? It cannot remain an unanalysed notion for the Predicate Nominalist. He might say that the type 'white' is simply the class of its tokens. This, however, is to change theories in mid-regress, and become a Class Nominalist about 'white'. If he is to remain a Predicate Nominalist, then he must say that all the tokens are of this type because they fall under a higher-order predicate "white". But this new predicate is again a type. The regress is infinite. Since reference to an unanalysed type always appears on the right-hand side of the analysis, the regress is vicious. But even if it were not vicious it would be uneconomical. In place of the original type, we substitute an infinite series of predicate-types, 'white', "white" . . . Better to have stayed with the original type, white. (Acceptance of this original type is sometimes attacked by Nominalists as uneconomical!)

The Relation regress is equally deadly. If we consider all those pairs consisting of (a) an object, and (b) a predicate which applies to the object; then the Predicate Nominalist cannot deny (because he asserts) that all these pairs have "something in common". They are all tokens of the common relation-type *falling under*. But the only account which he can consistently give of this situation is that all these pairs fall under the two-place predicate 'falling under'. The introduction of this new predicate involves a further Object regress, but this we may ignore. The Relation regress arises from the fact that the analysis involves once again the relation-type of *falling under*, a relation which links the pairs with the two-place predicate.

These new instances of *falling under* are either a different type of relation from the relation which holds between the original particulars and the original predicates, or they are the same type. If they are a different type then, in consistency, the analysis in terms of pairs of objects falling under a predicate must involve yet another, still higher-order type of *falling under*, which, however, again cannot be left unanalysed. This regress is certainly vicious.

If the new instances of *falling under* are of the same types as the original instances, there is no regress of different types. But still the regress seems vicious. The right-hand side of the analysis always proceeds in terms of certain objects falling under certain predicates. The Predicate Nominalist is therefore never able to remove the type-notion of *falling under* from his analyses. But since he professed to give a reductive analysis of all type-notions, his account is involved in circularity. And even if the regress were not vicious, it would involve the Predicate Nominalist in manifest lack of ontological economy.

What the two infinite regresses bring out is that the Predicate Nominalist does not in fact solve his problem, he simply shifts it. He is like a man who presses down the bulge in a carpet only to have it reappear elsewhere. Or he is like a man without funds who writes a cheque to cover his debts. When this is challenged he is prepared to write another cheque to cover the first cheque: and so for ever. He may postpone the evil day but he does not meet his debts.

v *Predicates and possible predicates*

In putting forward the infinite regress arguments against Predicate Nominalism, it was tacitly conceded to the Nominalist that he had available to him an infinite stock of predicates. Only so could he provide higher-order predicates in terms of which he could analyse what it is for predicates to be tokens of the same predicate-type.

But at some point in the regress, the Predicate Nominalist will run out of actual predicates. For a Nominalist, a predicate of a certain type can exist only if tokens of that type exist. Of course, the tokens need not exist currently. His existential quantifier need not assert current existence. $(\exists x)(\text{Dodo } x)$ is a true proposition. So, quite likely, is $(\exists x)(\text{Man on Mars } x)$. But, for a Nominalist, a predicate-type demands tokens which exist at *some* time.

Tokens may be lacking at the very first step. It is clearly possible, and we believe it to be the case, that particulars have certain properties and relations which never fall under human notice. Even where actual predicate-tokens exist for properties and relations, there will not in general be higher-order tokens under which these tokens fall. And even where there are such higher-order tokens, a very few steps up the ladder will ensure that we reach predicate-tokens which are of a certain type but do not fall under any actual predicates.

What is the Predicate Nominalist to do? At this point it is worth remembering our first criticism of Predicate Nominalism. A simple thought-experiment showed that a particular would still be white even if the predicate 'white' did not exist. The Predicate Nominalist could meet both that difficulty and the present one if he modified his analysis to:

> a has the property, F, if and only if
> a falls under a *possible* predicate 'F'.

This gets the Predicate Nominalist out of two frying-pans but lands him in a very hot fire. How is the new formula to be understood? Is the Predicate Nominalist committing himself to *entities* called 'possible predicates'? This may not contradict the letter of Nominalism but certainly contradicts its spirit. Types are traded off for *possibilia*, with all their paradoxes and difficulties.

If the Predicate Nominalist is not willing to postulate *possibilia*, then his analysis amounts to saying that *a* exists and that a certain hypothetical proposition is true of *a*, *viz.* if there were a predicate 'F', then *a* would fall under it. But what is it in the world which makes the hypothetical proposition true? To postulate hypothetical states of affairs resurrects the ontology of *possibilia*. But what other answer can be given except that the object *a* has a certain *nature* which would serve as ground for applying the predicate 'F' if there were such a predicate? Yet to give this answer is to abandon Predicate Nominalism. We should then require an account of this nature which *a* has, and the account cannot be given in terms of possibility.[1]

vi *Predicate Nominalism and causality*

The next argument depends upon three premisses. First, there are causes in nature. Second, the causal order is independent of the classifications which we make. Third, what causes what depends solely upon the properties (including relational properties) of the cause and the effect. From this it follows that properties are inde-

[1] Quine (1960, pp. 194–5) offers a typically ingenious, but typically artificial, solution of the problem of linguistic expressions which lack any tokens. But his solution depends upon giving *classes* a special ontological status. The latter doctrine will be criticized in ch. 4 § 1.

pendent of the classifications which we make, and thus that the Predicate Nominalist's account of properties is false.

The connection between causation and properties is probably the most controversial premiss of this argument. But even this premiss is generally acknowledged. If a stone hits a piece of glass and the glass shatters, then what occurs is thought to depend wholly upon what sort of thing the stone is, what sort of state it is in (for instance, its state of motion), what sort of thing and what state the glass is in, and what sort of circumstances surround the encounter of stone and glass. If stone, glass and environment had had certain other properties, then the outcome would have been a different sort of outcome from what in fact it was.

This link between a cause and its effect, on the one hand, and the nature of that cause and its effect, on the other, is made explicit in one theory of causation: the Humean or Regularity view. On this analysis it makes no sense to speak of one thing or event causing another unless this sequence is such that, on other occasions, the same *sort* of antecedent, in the same *sort* of circumstances, is always succeeded by the same *sort* of consequent. A Regularity view is not committed to any particular philosophy of properties, but it is committed to the view that one thing causes another by virtue of its properties. But if it is also granted that causal sequences exist as causal sequences independently of our classifications of them, then the Humean must reject Predicate Nominalism.

A Humean about causation *must* link causality with properties, though he need not give a Realist account of properties. But even if we reject a Humean view of causality (as I believe we should) it is utterly natural to think that what causes what is determined by the properties of the things (events) involved.

There is one analysis of causation which rejects this connection: it is the Singularist view developed by Elizabeth Anscombe (1971). According to this view, in a causal sequence it is a particular event *qua* particular which brings about a further particular event. Hume held that it is logically possible that anything should be the cause of anything, but he did stipulate that to be accounted "cause" and "effect" the particulars involved must be instances of a regular sequence. But on the Singularist view even the demand for regularity is dropped from the concept of causation. Unlike the Humean view, there is then no logical connection between the notion of cause and the notion of a law of nature.

I do not know how, if at all, a Singularist theory of causation is to be refuted, although I find it quite unbelievable. I have mentioned it here because it is the only account of causation of which I am aware which denies the connection between causation and properties. But once a Singularist theory of causation is rejected we are committed to saying that whatever is a cause acts causally in virtue of its properties. If it is accepted further that causal relations are objective and do not depend upon our classifications, then Predicate Nominalism must be an unsatisfactory account of what it is for a thing to have a property.

3
Concept Nominalism

Once the difficulties for Predicate Nominalism are appreciated, no very extensive examination of Concept Nominalism is required.

The Concept Nominalist calls upon concepts, conceived as mental entities, to do the same job for which the Predicate Nominalist employs predicates. The Concept Nominalist gives as his analysis of a's being F the statement that a falls under the concept F. Since concepts are mental entities, tokens of the concept F are found in men's minds. But a's being F is a matter of the concept-*type* being applicable to a. (We can say that concept-tokens are tokens of the same concept-type if and only if the intentional objects of the tokens are identical.)

Predicate and Concept Nominalism may be said to be the two *Subjectivist* solutions to the Problem of Universals. In one case universality is located in men's words, in the other case in men's minds. But in both cases man is the measure. Predicate Nominalism looks to an outward and visible thing: the linguistic expression. Its bias may be said to be Behaviourist. Concept Nominalism, by contrast, has a Mentalist bias.

Concepts are a more mysterious sort of entity than linguistic expressions, and extreme Behaviourists have even denied their existence. A less extreme Behaviourism has identified concepts with capacities or dispositions to wield predicates. Other philosophers have identified concepts with images which have a representative function or with capacities and/or dispositions to have such images. I think that there are conclusive reasons for rejecting all these accounts of concepts and, if this is correct, the difficulty of finding a satisfactory account of the nature of concepts may be thought to be some embarrassment for the Concept Nominalist.

However, I think that an adequate theory of concepts as mental entities can be developed (for an attempt see Armstrong, 1973, ch. 5 especially), and that it is concepts which underlie and give life to predicates rather than the other way about. But in any case, the

Concept Nominalist need do no more than take as primitive the notions of a concept as a mental entity and that of a thing falling under a concept.

Aaron (1939) has argued, correctly I think, that classical discussions of the problem of universals, particularly in the British Empiricist tradition, have often confused two questions: (*a*) what are concepts and how do they apply to the things which fall under them; and (*b*) what constitutes the unity of a class of things which are all said to have the same property or be of one sort or kind. The second of these problems is the ontological problem of universals which is the concern of this work.

The relation between the two problems is a trifle ambiguous. If Concept Nominalism is true, then, of course, to solve the first problem is to solve the second. But if it is not true, then the problems may have to be solved independently. For instance, our solution to the second problem, the problem of universals, might do little or nothing to cast light upon the nature of concepts and what it is for them to be applicable to particulars. Even if Concept Nominalism is true, and both problems have the same solution, it is still important to distinguish the problems.

The tendency of philosophers to confuse the two problems is shown by the way that many speak indifferently of "an instance falling under the concept of whiteness" and "an instance of whiteness". Any instance of the one will be an instance of the other, but, unless Concept Nominalism is correct, the two phrases do not mean the same thing. And if Concept Nominalism is true, its truth must be argued for explicitly, not simply assumed by our way of speaking.

The "British Empiricists", Locke, Berkeley and Hume, are often taken to be Concept Nominalists. It is not clear to what extent this is so. What *is* clear is that they had views about what concepts are (though they spoke of "ideas") and how concepts apply to the things which fall under them. But did they think that their theories of concepts were solutions to the ontological problem of universals? They certainly had a bias towards Concept Nominalism, and they seem to have thought that their discussions of the nature of concepts threw some light on what it is for a thing to have a property or for things to have a certain relation. More than this cannot safely be said. I have the impression that they never got the ontological problem into clear focus.

So much for preliminary remarks about Concept Nominalism.

The difficulties it faces seem to be exactly the same as those encountered by Predicate Nominalism. We may therefore be brief.

First, it seems clear that the whiteness of a white thing is independent of the existence of a concept of whiteness in men's minds. There is something about a white thing which makes the concept of whiteness applicable to it. Concept Nominalism gives no account of this something.

Second, the Concept Nominalist analysis involves two vicious infinite regresses. The concept of whiteness under which all white things fall is the concept considered as a type. Tokens of this concept can only be considered tokens of this type if they fall under the concept of the concept of white, and so on. Again, *falling under* is a type of relation. Pairs of particulars and concepts can only be considered tokens of this type if they fall under the concept *falling under*. But this new *falling under* again requires analysis.

Third, the Concept Nominalist must run out of actual tokens of concept-types to perform the required unification of classes of particulars. In the case of properties and relations of which no rational being is ever aware, concepts will be lacking from the very beginning. The Concept Nominalist will then have to appeal to possible but unactualized concepts with all the ontological difficulties which this appeal involves.

Fourth, the Concept Nominalist faces a problem about causality. The causal order of the world depends upon the properties of things. Again, the causal order is, in general, independent of the minds which take account of it. But, inconsistently, the Concept Nominalist holds that the properties of things are determined by a certain relation which things in the world have to objects in minds.

4
Class Nominalism

The unsatisfactory nature of the Subjectivist analyses, that is to say Predicate and Concept Nominalism, prompts us to consider Objectivist solutions where an account of a thing's having a property or thing's standing in a relation is given in terms which involve no reference to human classifications. All the proposed solutions to the Problem of Universals still to be considered are Objectivist solutions. It would therefore be natural to speak of them as "Realistic" solutions if that term had not been appropriated by a sub-class of the Objectivist solutions: those which postulate objective *universals*.[1]

The first Objectivist (and third Nominalist) suggestion to be examined is the view that *a*'s having a property, F, should be analysed as *a*'s being a member of a certain class of things, the class of Fs. The phrase "the class of Fs" must, of course, be 'taken in extension'. For the Class Nominalist the phrase is simply a convenient way of picking out a certain class of particulars. Otherwise his analysis is involved in blatant circularity.

As I mentioned in ch. 2, it is difficult to find a philosopher who explicitly defends Class Nominalism. G. E. Moore (1953, based on lectures given in 1911) states the view and expresses some sympathy with it. He considers *being a space*, but clearly intends what he says to apply to properties generally. He says that it is:

> Tempting and natural to suggest that *the* property which is common and peculiar to *all* spaces, is ... that each of them is a member of the group consisting of all spaces. (p. 314)

Aside from this quotation, I have found only casual adoption of the class view in particular contexts.

What of relations? It is common to meet the assertion that a relation is nothing but a class of ordered pairs. *Monogamous marriage*, for instance, is the class of all ordered pairs consisting of

[1] H. H. Price (1953, p. 23) notes this point for the particular case of Resemblance Nominalism.

married couples. However, the notion of an *ordered* pair seems still to involve unreduced relations. Following Kuratowski, logicians therefore use a device which reduces the ordered pair, $\langle a, b \rangle$, to an unordered class of unordered classes, $\{\{a\} \{a,b\}\}$. If this device is treated as a serious piece of metaphysics, then we have a thorough-going Class Nominalism for relations. It does, of course, demand classes of higher type, that is, classes of classes.

One attraction of Class Nominalism is that the theory of classes is well-developed, which is not the case for the theory of properties. Quine says that the identity-conditions for classes are "crystal-clear" while the identity-conditions for properties are "obscure". One inference that might be drawn from this is that we should try to explain what it is for a thing to have a certain property in terms of its membership of a certain class.

In fact, however, there are many desperate difficulties for a Class Nominalism. Some, but only some, of these difficulties are much the same as those faced by Predicate and Concept Nominalism.

1 *Class Nominalism is committed to an ontology of classes*

Predicate and Concept Nominalism appeal in their analyses to entities – predicates and concepts – which almost every philosopher will concede to exist, at least as tokens. Predicates and concepts may not do the job which Predicate and Concept Nominalists hope that they do, but their existence is not in serious doubt. The contrast here is with Platonic Realism which tried to solve the Problem of Universals by postulating or claiming to discover entities about which there must be the greatest doubt.

In this respect the Class Nominalist is in an ambiguous position. There seems nothing very mysterious or metaphysical about classes. There is surely such a thing as the class of men. Neverthe-less, as classes are employed by the Class Nominalist, they do become mysterious entities because they have to be treated as entities different from the aggregate or heap of the members of these classes.

The Class Nominalist's need to distinguish classes from aggre-gates is brought out by the following example. Suppose that each thing of the sort F is made up of Gs and that Gs are not found except as proper parts of Fs. No Fs themselves are Gs. For instance, armies are wholly made up of soldiers, and soldiers are not found (we may say) except as parts of armies. Armies are not themselves soldiers. '*a* is an army' is analysed by the Class Nominalist as '*a* is a member of the class of armies', while '*b* is a soldier' is analysed as '*b* is a member of the class of soldiers'. Now consider the consequences for these analyses if classes are identical with the aggregate of their members. The aggregate of all armies is identical with the aggregate of all soldiers. Hence the class of all armies is identical with the class of all soldiers. So, by substitution, it is true that *a* (an army) is a member of the class of soldiers, and hence is a soldier. *b* (a soldier) is in the same way proved to be an army. These results are absurd. The Class Nominalist must therefore distinguish three things: the class of armies, the class of soldiers, the aggregate of armies (= the aggregate of soldiers). Classes and aggregates are distinct things.

The ontological commitment of the Class Nominalist may also be brought out by considering cases where an object has a certain property but it is the only object which has that property. Suppose that *a* is (omnitemporally) the only thing which is F. (But let it be the case that it is an intelligible notion that there are other things which are F. It will be argued at a later point that this is a necessary condition for something being a property.) It was pointed out in the discussion of Predicate and Concept Nominalism that a difficulty arises where *a* is F but there exists no actual predicate or concept in terms of which the analysis of *a*'s being F can proceed. A similar difficulty may appear to exist in the case of Class Nominalism where *a* is the only thing which is F. For then, it may be said, there is no class of Fs. However, this difficulty is met by introducing *unit*-classes. If *a* is F, yet nothing else is F, then *a* is still said to be a member of the class of Fs, but the class in question is a unit-class. So, although appropriate predicates and concepts may be lacking, appropriate classes never are.

But although the manœuvre yields this advantage over Predicate and Concept Nominalism, what is then very clear is the ontological commitment of Class Nominalism. For these unit-classes must be treated with ontological seriousness. The object *a* and the unit-class of Fs of which *a* is the sole member must be different entities. For suppose that *a* and the unit-class {a} are the very same thing. In what way then can *a*'s being F be *explained* by saying that *a* is a member of this unit-class?

But this ontological commitment is an ontological embarrassment. How implausible to say that accompanying every object which is, as a matter of fact, the sole instance of a property there is, automatically and inevitably, a class! The connection looks too tight to be a real connection between distinct entities. It looks to be a case of "metaphysical double vision", of taking the same entity twice over. Furthermore, since orthodox set-theory recognized not only classes, but classes of classes (required in any case for relations), the object a will apparently be accompanied by an infinite cloud of entities: $\{a\}, \{\{a\}\}, \{\{\{a\}\}\} \ldots$

But it is not simply unit-classes which involve such multiplication. The extraordinary and incredible proliferation of entities which results when we countenance both objects and classes of objects in our ontology has been emphasized by Nelson Goodman, particularly in his paper "A World of Individuals" (1956). Taking classes ontologically, as entities over and above the corresponding aggregate, is indeed a prospect that should delight the *a priori* metaphysician. One starts with individuals, forms all the possible different classes of these, which yields many further entities, and then one goes on to classes of classes and so on upward to infinity. A sober Empiricist must be appalled by the way entities are so easily manufactured. By comparison, one can only be astounded at the moderation displayed by, say, the supporters of the Ontological argument.

One argument which can be brought against the distinction between objects and classes of objects is of a type to which there will be frequent recourse in this work. It is the argument from the lack of causal power. If the aggregate of persons in this room and the class of persons in this room really are two different entities, then we should expect them to have different causal powers. If they do not, there would seem to be no reason to postulate both. In particular, if the class does no work in the world, over and above the work done by the aggregate, why postulate it in addition to the aggregate? The phenomena will be the same whether the class is there or not.

But to all these arguments the Class Nominalist may retort that, like it or not and whether or not we accept Class Nominalism, the distinction between an aggregate and the corresponding class is forced upon us. Even the opponent of Class Nominalism must admit that a is an army if and only if a is a member of the class of armies and b is a soldier if and only if b is a member of the class of soldiers. But if the class of armies = the aggregate of armies = the aggregate of soldiers = the class of soldiers, then a is an army if and only if a is a member of the class of soldiers. Which is absurd.

Again, if *a* is a member of a class, and that class is a member of a wider class, *a* is not necessarily a member of that wider class. Class-membership is not necessarily transitive. But if *a* is a part of an aggregate, and that aggregate is part of a larger aggregate, *a* must be a part of the wider aggregate.

Yet again, we can attach a number to the class of soldiers and to the class of armies. But no number can be attached to the corresponding aggregates.

Finally, and following on from the previous point, classes are required for mathematics. In particular, not simply classes but higher-order classes are required for those vital portions of mathematics which are required for physics.

But if we are forced to postulate classes as distinct from aggregates in any case, then there can be no objection to the Class Nominalist using them for his own purposes.

The question, however, is whether these arguments really require that we postulate classes as entities over and above the aggregate of the members of the class. Certainly, we must be able to make sense of talk about classes, and exhibit the difference of this talk from talk about the corresponding aggregate. But this requirement would be met in an unmetaphysical way if the two styles of discourse were simply different ways of referring to the very same thing.

Max Black (1971) and, following him, Erik Stenius (1974) have made what I think is a very important suggestion. They urge that when we refer to a class, but not when we refer to the corresponding aggregate, we are making a particular sort of *plural reference*. There is an unthinking tendency to assume that, when we use a referring expression, there is or purports to be a semantic correlation between the expression and just *one* something. But consider:

(1) Tom, Dick and Harry lifted a girder.
(2) Tom, Dick and Harry went to a party.

On the natural interpretation of (1) the phrase 'Tom, Dick and Harry' refers to a single entity: the team which Tom, Dick and Harry made up for the purpose of lifting the girder. In (2), however, the phrase 'Tom, Dick and Harry' is a plural referring phrase which saves us having to say or write:

(2′) Tom went to the party and Dick went to the party and Harry went to the party.

Black's and Stenius' suggestion is that phrases like 'the class of Fs' is more like the referring expression in (2) than in (1). It does not refer to a single entity, but is rather a plural referring expression, referring to each of the Fs, preparatory to saying that something is true of each of them. (I do not think, however, that when we ascribe a number to a class we are using a plural referring expression. To say that the class of Fs numbers 17 seems to be to say that the *aggregate* of the Fs is made up of 17 Fs. It is noteworthy that it is not very natural linguistically to 'ascribe a number' to a class. See ch. 18 §v.)

What recommends the Black–Stenius suggestion (but will probably be a stumbling-block to many logicians and philosophers) is its utter simplicity and naturalness. Those who draw a distinction in the world between aggregates and classes offer us the picture portrayed in figure 1.

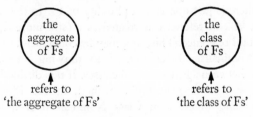

Fig. 1

This looks like metaphysical reduplication. By contrast, Black and Stenius suggest that we simplify our ontology by a little complication in our semantics. Figure 2 presents the picture for the case where there are just 3 Fs.

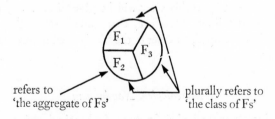

Fig. 2

What 'the aggregate of Fs' refers to is then seen to be the very same thing as the sum of things which 'the class of Fs' plurally refers to.

As I have said, the suggestion seems immensely attractive.

Unfortunately, however, I lack the expertise to defend it in depth and to show that it can account for all the differences in our talk about aggregates and classes. The vital question will be whether the suggestion can give a satisfactory account of *classes of classes* and higher-order classes generally. Such classes are essential for mathematics. Stenius objects to what Black says about classes of classes, but thinks nevertheless that the problem can be solved.

It does follow from this view that every genuine class has at least two members. What then of the unit-class and the null-class? They would have to be interpreted as mere symbolic devices introduced for convenience by set-theorists to deal with certain "degenerate" cases. In the case of an object and its unit-class, both styles of reference are really singular. But, by speaking of unit-classes, singular reference is treated as a (degenerate) case of plural reference. This will have its utility, particularly in cases where it is not known whether there is just one F or a plurality of Fs. In the case of the null-class, lack of reference is treated as a (still more degenerate) case of plural reference. This, too, may be convenient.

Class Nominalism is committed to drawing an ontological distinction between aggregates and classes. If this distinction can be otherwise and more plausibly explained, in the Black–Stenius fashion or any other, then Class Nominalism is in difficulty. Suppose, however, that we are forced to distinguish ontologically between aggregates and classes. Even then, as we shall see, there remain plenty of arguments strong enough to refute Class *Nominalism*. But in any case, if we go on to take a Realistic view of properties and relations, then it seems ontological extravagance to recognize classes as *additional* entities to properties and relations. (Arguments to support this view will be given in ch. 12.) I shall assume in what follows, therefore, that some form of "no-class" theory can be developed, whether in the Black–Stenius manner or in some other.

11 *Mereological Nominalism*

At this point we may take brief note of the heroic doctrine which I have called Mereological Nominalism. It tries to give an account of what it is for a thing to have a property not in terms of classes but of aggregates. *a* is F if and only if *a* is a part (proper or otherwise) of the aggregate of all the Fs. Bochenski (1956, p. 47) appropriately calls it the "bit" theory. *a* is F because it is a bit of the great F thing. The theory must be distinguished from that crude version of the theory of Forms which puts a bit of the Form F in each particular which is F (see Plato, *Parmenides*, 131 b–c), an over-literal form of *universalia in rebus*. Mereological Nominalism admits only particulars, standing to each other in the relation of part and whole.

The obvious advantage of the theory is that it avoids appeal to an ontology of classes. Its obvious disadvantage is that, while it is a necessary condition of *a*'s being F that *a* is a part of the aggregate of Fs, it is not, in general, sufficient. It has some plausibility to say that *each* part of the aggregate of white things is white. But it is false that each part of the aggregate of things having the mass of one kilogram has the mass of one kilogram. Most of such parts have a different mass. This is the case for most properties, and, scientific investigation may perhaps reveal, even for all properties. Again, there can be few if any relations such that, given the aggregate of the things related by that *n*-adic relation, *any n* parts of that aggregate will be related by that same relation.

But even in the case of a putative property such as *whiteness*, it is clear that the theory is inadequate. To mention only one difficulty, it is not the case that a white thing derives its whiteness from being a part of the great white aggregate. Rather, inspection reveals, it belongs to the aggregate of white things *because it is white*.

III *Class Nominalism and co-extensive properties*

This is the really notorious weakness of Class Nominalism, the one with which every philosopher is familiar. Classes are identical if and only if they have identical members. It seems possible, however, that there could be two distinct properties, F and G, which are co-extensive. But the class of Fs will be the very same class as the class of Gs, and so, if Class Nominalism is true, the propositions that *a* is F and that *a* is G will be identical properties, which is contrary to hypothesis. A particular application of the difficulty arises in the case where nothing is F and nothing is G. F and G then have the same extension – the null-class – and so F and G must be the very same property.

It should be noticed that this difficulty can be met if Class Nominalism is combined with an ontology of possible worlds. Suppose that F and G are co-extensive properties in the actual world. Nevertheless, in general there will be *possible* worlds in which there are Fs which are not Gs and Gs which are not Fs. 'Fa' can then be analysed as '*a* is a member of the class of all possible Fs' and 'Ga' as '*a* is a member of the class of all possible Gs'. *These* two classes will not be co-extensive. The only exception will be the case where F and G are co-extensive of logical necessity. But it is plausible to suggest that in that exceptional case F and G are the very same property.

In this way, the objection to Class Nominalism from co-extensive properties can be circumvented. But the Nominalist may well consider that if Class Nominalism can only be defended by embracing an ontology of possible worlds, then the remedy is worse than the disease.

It will be noted in ch. 8 that the difficulty can also be met if the properties of particulars are taken to be themselves particulars. For the phrases "the class of Fs" and "the class of Gs" can then be given an interpretation which makes them distinct classes.

iv *Can class-membership determine properties?*

The third argument against Class Nominalism is the same as the first argument brought against Predicate and Concept Nominalism. *a*'s being a member of the class of Fs is, presumably, a matter of a *relation* holding between *a* and the class. It may be compared to the relation which *a* has to the predicate-type 'F', or the concept *F*, relations which are exploited by Predicate and Concept Nominalism respectively. But, just as in these two other cases, it seems intuitively clear that the relation does not *constitute a*'s being F but rather depends upon *a*'s being F.

One way of bringing out this point is to consider that the class of Fs may be an infinite one. For any finite mind, therefore, there will be Fs which are unknown to it. Suppose, then, that this mind comes upon an object with which it has no previous acquaintance, and the question arises whether or not the object belongs to the class of Fs. The decision must be based upon the nature of the object. But, given Class Nominalism, to say it has that nature is only to say it is a member of the class of Fs. It seems obvious, however, that we could use the thing's nature to determine whether or not it belongs to the class of Fs. So its nature is not constituted by membership of the class of Fs.

Another way of bringing out the point is to make the same thought-experiment which we made in the case of Predicate Nominalism. Consider a particular white thing. It is a member of the class of white things; and according to the Class Nominalist its whiteness is constituted by membership of that class. But now imagine that the remainder of the class does not exist. The white thing will be left alone with its unit-class. But may it not still be white? So the remainder of the class has nothing to do with its whiteness.[1]

Before ending this section I will anticipate a point in the positive theory of universals. It is a *necessary* condition of P being a property that there be no limits *in logic* to the number of things which are P. The number of particulars which are P may be finite, or it may be infinite. Under these conditions, the class of Ps, specified as the class of Ps, may be said to be an "open" or "unrestricted" class. (Although it is a necessary condition of P's being a property that the class of Ps, specified as the class of Ps, be an open class, we shall see later when we come to develop the theory of universals in volume II that it is insufficient.)

Now it is, of course, open classes which create difficulties for the Class Nominalist. Consider, by way of contrast, a case where a class, as specified, is not an open class. Perhaps it is specified as the class containing the members *a, b, c, d*. Consider now the "property", *being a or b or c or d*. The Class Nominalist analysis of this "property" would be perfectly correct. The necessary and sufficient conditions for having this "property" would be being a member of the class {a, b, c, d}. However, I would deny that *being a or b or c or d* is really a property.

v *An argument from the identity-conditions for classes*

The next argument is a close relative of the previous one. It is due to Wolterstorff (1970, ch. 8). In § IV it was pointed out that the class of white things might be different, yet the *whiteness* of a white thing be unaffected. Hence the class of white things is irrelevant to the *whiteness* of the white thing. It must now be pointed out that, if the class of white things is different, then, given the Class analysis, the *whiteness* of the white thing must be affected.

Suppose, for instance, that there were other white things besides

[1] The point is noted by Ayer (1971), p. 71.

the ones which actually exist. The class is then a different class. For, as logicians insist, the condition of identity of a class is identity of membership. If the class has a different membership, then it is a different class. (Remember, again, that in the Class Nominalist analysis the phrase "the class of white things" must be 'taken in extension'.) Hence, under the new conditions, what it is for something to be white would have to change. But it is clear that it would not in fact change.

This argument would fail if a's being white were analysed not in terms of a's membership of the class of actual white things but in terms of its membership of the class of white things in all possible worlds. The desperate nature of such a remedy has already been noted.

VI *Only some classes are natural classes*

If our project is to give an account of properties (and relations) purely in terms of class-membership, then it will be necessary to take a completely egalitarian attitude towards classes, or at any rate towards all classes of particulars. It cannot be allowed that there are classes whose members have a common property while the members of other classes lack such a property. For it would be impossible to explain this difference purely in terms of a class analysis. This conclusion holds for finite as much as for infinite classes. For if P is a property, although it must be logically possible that the class of Ps is infinite in number, it may in fact be finite. Class Nominalism is therefore committed to the view that, necessarily, the members of every class of particulars have a common property just in virtue of being members of that class. Indeed, associated with each different class there must be a different property. This conclusion, however, is unacceptable. It may as a matter of fact be true, but there is no necessity that it be true.

It must be confessed, however, that there are some Nominalist philosophers who have simply accepted the conclusion that every class of particulars generates a property common to each member of the class. Stuart Hampshire (1950) wrote:

> Of any finite group of objects, however numerous and heterogeneous they may be, it is always meaningless to deny . . . that they all resemble each other in some one respect.

The omitted words are "—— and in that sense also meaningless to assert ——". But I take them to be a mere genuflection to Wittgensteinian doctrine that only what can be meaningfully denied can be meaningfully asserted.

I do not know how to argue against this heroic view except by asserting its implausibility and calling attention to three invalid lines of reasoning which may be helping to prop up the view in the minds of those who hold it.

First, it is clear that the properties of which we actually take notice are fewer than the properties which things actually have. The concepts and predicates which we actually employ are determined by our powers of discernment and our interests. They divide up the world in a certain way. Relative to this scheme, certain classes appear natural, others arbitrary. But it is easy to see that a different set of concepts and predicates, springing from different powers and interests, would make other classes natural and *our* natural classes arbitrary. These considerations may then generate the belief that, seen ontologically, any sorting at all of things into classes is as good as any other. In fact, however, it should be clear that this conclusion is invalidly drawn. The fact that there are many more property-classes than those picked out in ordinary discourse does not show that every class is a property-class.

Second, given any finite class, at least, it will always be logically possible to manufacture a *predicate* which applies to each member of the class, if only of the form 'is *a*, or is *b*, or is . . .'. It is then tempting to reason from the possibility of a predicate to the reality of a property. In fact, however, as we noted in §IV, and will argue in detail in Part Four, it is not the case that every predicate applies to the particulars it applies to in virtue of some property.

Third, it may be that some philosophers are swayed by an analogy from mathematics. Given any finite set of integers, whether a natural or an unnatural looking set, there exists a formula which will generate this set and go on to generate an indefinite number of further integers. Perhaps some thinkers (I have in mind particularly Wittgenstein in the *Investigations*) have taken this situation as a model for the bringing of arbitrary sets of particulars under common properties.

In fact, however, the analogy does not carry through. Each different integer is different in nature from every other integer; differences, however, which are based on definite similarities. The similarities enable us to find things which members of any set of integers have in common. But when the Class-membership analysis tries to assert that members of any class of particulars have a common property, there is no guarantee that there will be such similarities to work upon. Of course the Class Nominalist can change his analysis by stipulating that not every class generates a property, but only those whose members exhibit similarities. But then he is trying to bolster the Class analysis with a Resemblance theory.

Against Hampshire, the natural view to take seems to be that not every class of particulars need be associated with a property. There can be, and no doubt are, indefinitely heterogeneous classes. (By contrast, it will be argued later on that every property picks out a class, even if only a unit-class.) Pure Class Nominalism, however, can give no account of the distinction between a property-class and a heterogeneous class.

Anthony Quinton (1957 and 1973, ch. 9) recognizes this problem for Class Nominalism and espouses what may be called a Moderate Class Nominalism. For him it is an ultimate or brute fact that some classes of particulars form "natural" classes while others do not. For *a* to have the property, F, is for *a* to be a member of the natural class of Fs. The distinction between natural and non-natural classes he takes to be a matter of degree. There are some classes such that, if somebody is presented with some of their members, he can very easily go on and pick out further members. The class of blue things would be a case in point. For other classes the same task might be very difficult. An example would be the class of things which are not blue. Presented with heterogeneous things which had nothing in common except their lack of blueness, it would not be easy to catch on to their "common property". There would be intermediate cases where the task of picking out the further individuals would be of intermediate difficulty.

Quinton's view is not without elements of Predicate or Concept Nominalism, because he makes possession of a property to be a notion relative to the classification of things which we (naturally) make. At the same time, he does seem to hold that there is an *ontological* distinction between natural and non-natural classes. But it is difficult for him to maintain that this ontological distinction is fundamentally a distinction between *classes*. For instance, given a certain member of a certain natural class, it would seem obvious that it is the nature of the member which makes it a member of the class, rather than its class-membership which bestows that nature upon it (see § IV again). If this is so, Quinton still owes us an account of the *nature* of individuals. Indeed, Quinton's view faces all the difficulties we are bringing against Class Nominalism except the difficulty that not all classes are associated with a property. And even this difficulty he has met only by complicating his ontology with the introduction of natural classes.

VII *Class Nominalism and two infinite regresses*

In ch. 2 § IV it was argued that Predicate Nominalism is involved in two vicious infinite regresses, christened the "Object" and the "Relation" regress respectively. Two similar regresses threaten in the case of Class Nominalism. I will argue that there is no Object regress in the case of Class Nominalism but that the Relation regress obtains and is vicious.

One may attempt to develop the Object regress in the following way. Consider the object that is the class of Fs. (This is the equivalent of the predicate 'F' or the concept F in the case of Predicate and Concept Nominalism.) To say that it is the class of Fs tells us the nature of the class. So it appears to attribute a property to the class. Hence, it may be argued, a Class Nominalist must in consistency give a class-membership analysis of the attribution of this property. A unit-class must therefore be invoked of which the class of Fs is a member. But then the same problem breaks out in the case of this unit-class, and so *ad infinitum*.

This argument is interestingly fallacious. The problem of universals is the problem of how numerically different particulars can nevertheless be identical in nature, all be of the same "type". This is why it was said in §IV that it is a necessary condition of P's being a property that it is logically possible that the number of Ps is infinite. But what makes the class of Fs to be the class of Fs is not something which any object besides that class could possess. It is a "property" which is necessarily unique to the class of Fs.

The point may be put in semantic terms. The phrases "the class of Fs" and "all the Fs" are *referring* expressions. (Black and Stenius maintain that they are plural referring expressions.) Predicate and Concept Nominalists relate particulars to predicate- and concept-*types* respectively. In this way they give themselves a new problem.

But the Class Nominalist relates particulars to something unrepeatable, something not a type: a particular class. So against Class Nominalism the Object regress cannot get started.

The Relation regress is a different matter, however. Class Nominalism explains what it is for particulars to have properties by appealing to the relation of class-membership which these particulars have to various classes. Although properties can be treated as classes of particulars, and relations as certain classes of classes of particulars, Class Nominalism must employ one two-place predicate '———— $\in$ ————', that is 'being a member of '.[1] But what corresponds to this predicate is a certain type of relation whose tokens are all those ordered pairs consisting of, first, a particular or particulars and second, all those classes of which these particulars are members. The Class Nominalist, however, is committed to giving a reductive analysis of all types in terms of particulars. Hence the Class Nominalist is forced to attempt a Class analysis of the class membership relation.

It is easy to see, however, that this attempt must be involved in a vicious regress. *a*'s being F is analysed as *a*'s being a member of the class of Fs. If *being a member of* must also be analysed, it will be a matter of the ordered pair consisting of *a* and the class of Fs *being a member of* the class of all those ordered pairs which "stand in the relation of class-membership". But then a type-notion of *being a member of* has reappeared unanalysed in the analysis. Whether this is declared to be a new type (higher-order class-membership) or the very same type as before, it is clear that the attempt to remove unanalysed type-notions from the right-hand side of the analysis has failed.

I conclude, therefore, that the Relation regress does hold against Class Nominalism.

VIII *Class Nominalism and causality*

We have noted that in a causal relationship the particulars which enter into it produce whatever sort of effect they produce in virtue solely of the *properties* of the particulars (ch. 2 § VI). For the Class Nominalist, a particular has a property if it is a member of a certain "open", perhaps infinite, class. Suppose, now, that a certain particular brings about certain effects in virtue of the fact that it has

[1] A point noted by Küng (1967), p. 28 n. 16.

a certain mass, say two kilograms. On the Class analysis, the possession of this property will be constituted by its membership of the class of two-kilogram particulars. But what have all the other members of the class to do with the causal efficacy of this particular? If the particular operates on Earth, then its operation appears to be quite independent of the many two-kilogram particulars on Sirius! It carries its causal efficacy within itself. But if it also be granted that its causal efficacy depends upon its properties, then possession of any of these properties cannot be a matter of the particular being a member of a certain class of particulars, such as the class of two-kilogram particulars.

5

Resemblance Nominalism

I *The Resemblance analysis*

The trouble with a pure Class Nominalism is that there are too many classes of particulars. Each is as good as any other, and so each must be allowed to generate its own property. Some Nominalists have simply embraced this conclusion, but it is not a comfortable one to accept. It would be preferable to allow that classes of particulars may or may not have a common property. But how are particulars to be brought together *selectively*? We have already investigated and discarded the suggestion that this be done by bringing them under a common predicate or concept. Quinton's "natural" classes seem more a statement than a solution of the problem. The suggestion now to be considered is that it be done by means of relations of resemblance between the particulars.

Consider a number of things which "have the same property". It follows that they all resemble each other, in some degree at least. The resemblance may appear to flow from this common property. But we can instead try taking the resemblance as primitive and analyse "the common property" in terms of the resemblance which the particulars bear to each other. The foundation for our sortings and classifyings will then be found in "the similitudes in things". If we agree that these resemblances exist independently of their being perceived, conceived or predicated, then the foundation is objective.

However, the appeal to resemblance runs into an immediate difficulty. If we consider the predicate 'white' or the mental concept of whiteness or the Platonic Form of Whiteness, then it is clear that they can be used to mark off the class of white things from all other things. Perhaps these entities do not really do anything to help solve the Problem of Universals. But at least the predicate and the concept apply to all and only white things, and, if there is such a thing as the Form of Whiteness, all and only the white things participate in it.

But although each white thing has a resemblance to each other white thing, there may well be a class which includes the class of white things, yet where each member of this wider class resembles every other member. It may even, though it need not, be the case that everything resembles everything else. Mere resemblance, therefore, will not serve to mark off white things from all other things. The Realist has a simple explanation for this superfluity of resemblance. He says that if *a* resembles *b*, then there is a respect, C, such that *a* is C and *b* is C. White things resemble each other in respect of whiteness, but a white thing may well resemble a non-white thing in some other respect. These respects appear to be universals. So, the Realist will say, resemblance is so far from providing an alternative to universals that it actually presupposes them.

And, indeed, the Resemblance Nominalist cannot deny that we often speak of things as resembling each other in a certain respect and that it is very convenient to speak in this way. But he must deny that resemblance can be *analysed* in terms of sameness of respect. He will try to avoid such an analysis, and overcome the difficulty created by the superfluity of resemblance, by appealing (a) to the notion of *degrees of resemblance*; and (b) to the notion of *paradigms*.

We do speak of degrees of resemblance. We say that *a* resembles *b* more than *a* resembles *c*, or that *a* resembles *b* more than *c* resembles *d*. Degree of resemblance has a theoretical upper limit in complete resemblance, and a theoretical lower limit in complete lack of resemblance. It has been maintained that both these limits are unreachable, but that question need not detain us for the present.

(We speak of degree of resemblance not only of particulars but also of universals. We say, for instance, that *redness* resembles *orangeness* more than *redness* resembles *blueness*. In the next chapter it will be argued that such resemblances create insuperable difficulties for all varieties of orthodox Nominalism. At a much later stage (Part Six), a positive theory of such resemblance will be put forward. But our present concern is with degrees of resemblance among *particulars*.)

Although we speak of degrees of resemblance, it might be maintained that such degrees are a relative matter, relative to the particular concepts or predicates employed. The Resemblance Nominalist, however, requires that degree of resemblance be objective. Given three particulars, *a*, *b* and *c*, he must maintain that it is an objective question, simply a matter of the way that the world is, whether *a* resembles *c* more than, less than or to the same degree as *b* resembles *c*. Only so can he hope to build up objective resemblance-classes.

Resemblance Nominalism must also employ the notion of certain *paradigm particulars*. The necessity for such paradigm objects is easy to see. Suppose, for instance, that we try to supply the uniting principle of the white things by saying that each of them resembles every other one more closely than any of them resemble anything else. The trouble then is that we wish to use the same formula to unite, say, the red things. What then differentiates white things from red things? The Resemblance theorist cannot appeal to their *whiteness* and *redness*! Paradigm particulars are introduced to solve this difficulty. White things have a suitable resemblance to *this* thing, red things a suitable resemblance to *that*.

Resemblance Nominalism was earlier described as an Objectivist analysis. But it should be noted that the appeal to paradigms introduces a certain element of subjectivity, or at least of relativity. For it is clear that different people will normally have to use different paradigms for the same class of things. To that extent, for the Resemblance theorists, whiteness for you is not the same thing as whiteness for me.

It may be noted further that in a passage where Quine considers, only to reject, a Resemblance analysis of what he calls "kinds" (1969, pp. 119–21), he makes no appeal to such particulars. (He does use the notion of "paradigms", but they are types, not tokens.) But he is able to do this because he takes kinds to be certain *classes* "determined by their members" (p. 118). The view he considers and rejects is thus a variety of Class Nominalism, exposed to the difficulties we have brought against Class Nominalism. It simply attempts to meet the difficulty that it is not necessary that all classes determine a property. But if the Resemblance Nominalist allows himself to begin with only particulars and degrees of resemblance between them, and on this basis tries to build up classes of things "having the same property", then he must appeal to paradigm particulars.

So much for preliminaries. As an example of an actual Resemblance analysis we may take that put forward by H. H. Price (1953, ch. 1).[1] For each class of things which "have the same property" he

---

[1] It should be noticed that Price argues that the Resemblance theory and the theory of Universals are nothing more than "alternative languages" for stating the same onto-

begins by requiring "a small group of standard objects or exemplars". For instance, the exemplars for red things might be "a certain tomato, a certain brick and a certain British post-box". He adds, however, that the one class may have alternative sets of exemplars: "a certain bit of sealing-wax, a certain blushing face and a certain sunset sky". As we have noticed, it will normally be the case that different people work with different sets of exemplars. Now, Price suggests, a red object is any object which resembles the exemplars as closely as the exemplars resemble one another:

> The resemblance between the exemplars need not itself be a very close one, though it is of course pretty close in the example just given. What is required is only that every other member of the class should resemble the class-exemplars *as* closely as they resemble one another. Thus the exemplars for a class might be a summer sky, a lemon, a post-box and a lawn. These do resemble one another, though not very closely. Accordingly there is a class consisting of everything which resembles these four entities *as* closely as they resemble each other. It is the class of coloured things . . . (p. 21)

"Resembling as closely as" must here be understood as "resembling *at least* as closely as". Furthermore, for other objects to be members of the class, they must resemble *each* of the paradigm objects as closely as each of the paradigm objects resembles each of the other paradigm objects. It will not be sufficient if the objects sufficiently resemble just one of the paradigms. For they might resemble that paradigm in what ordinary language would call "some quite irrelevant respect".

It may not be necessary to give this account of *all* "attributions of properties" (and "attributions of relations"). Provided that the epistemologically unanalysable universals were dealt with in this way, complex universals might be dealt with in terms of the unanalysable ones.

It will be seen that, unlike the first three varieties of Nominalism, the working out of a Resemblance analysis requires a good deal of honest toil. The complexity of Price's careful analysis is typical of what is demanded if the theory is to get beyond vague gestures.

---

logical facts. I think that Price is wrong here. For an excellent criticism of this "alternative language" view, see Raphael (1955).

Furthermore, the resulting theory does much better justice to important phenomena than any other Nominalism. Unfortunately, however, the resulting account seems just as vulnerable to a variety of criticisms as the other forms of Nominalism. I pass on to consider these difficulties.

II *Over-determination of the paradigms*

It is clearly possible that the paradigms or exemplars for one property-class should also serve as exemplars for another. Suppose, for instance, that the paradigms for the class of red things are also objects which have a very high density. The paradigms will then "collect" the class of things which either are red or are very dense. And so it will not follow that an object which resembles the paradigms for the red class at least as closely as the paradigms resemble each other is a red object. For it might be dense and not red.

Could we eliminate this difficulty simply by selecting suitable standard objects for which the awkward situation does not arise? The difficulty for the Resemblance Nominalist is that he is trying to give a logical analysis of what it is for something to have a certain property. Now, whatever paradigms are selected, it always remains possible that, over and above the property-class for which they are chosen to be paradigms, they will actually serve as paradigms for a quite distinct property-class. In the language of properties, they may have common properties over and above the one intended. But if this is so, it will need to be specified in the analysis that the paradigms must only be used as paradigms for the intended property. But how can this be done without bringing in that very notion of a property which was supposed to be analysed?

This difficulty is a difficulty for the particular suggestion put forward by Price. Nelson Goodman has put forward two difficulties of a similar sort for a construction of Carnap's (Carnap 1967, §§ 67–93 and 108–20; Goodman 1966, ch. 5 § III). The likelihood of such difficulties can be seen *a priori*. Like all Nominalist theories, the Resemblance analysis must treat each particular as a single un-differentiated whole. To sort out these particulars into a huge multitude of overlapping property-classes, the Resemblance theory has nothing more than a one-dimensional scale of degrees of resemblance. It is not surprising that the task exceeds the means available.

III *The symmetry of resemblance*

It is a necessary truth that, if a resembles b, then b resembles a. Necessarily, resemblance is symmetrical. But if resemblance is a fundamental notion, as the Resemblance Nominalist holds, then this necessary truth is a bed-rock and inexplicable fact.

The difficulty for the Resemblance Nominalist is that this necessary truth does not seem to be inexplicable at all. It is natural to derive the symmetry of resemblance from the symmetry of identity. a resembles b if and only if a and b are in some respect identical. There exists a respect, C, in which a and b are identical. The symmetry of C's identity with itself then ensures the symmetry of resemblance. But since the Resemblance Nominalist denies that when a and b resemble each other they are in any respect identical, this derivation of the symmetry of resemblance is not available to him. He must just accept it as a brute necessity. Since, furthermore, he must admit that there is such a thing as the identity of particulars, he also requires the notion of identity. His theory is therefore uneconomical. It multiplies necessities without necessity.

It may be noted, incidentally, that this argument seems not merely to be an argument against Resemblance Nominalism, but also to give positive support to Realism. For Realism about universals is the doctrine that there really is such a thing as a generic identity, identity of nature, which cannot be analysed away. Any theory which denies this may be challenged to explain the symmetry of resemblance.

Keith Campbell has pointed out that the Resemblance theorist can attempt to meet the charge of lack of economy in principles by giving an analysis of the identity of particulars in terms of resemblance. He can assert, intending it as a logical analysis of such identity, that a is identical with b if and only if a resembles b exactly. Two different particulars, he can say, necessarily fail of resemblance at some point. At the top of the resemblance-scale, the resembling things are necessarily one. The symmetry of identity is then derived from the symmetry of resemblance.

However, this attempt by the Resemblance Nominalist to even the score depends upon his being able to maintain that it is logically impossible for two things, in Realist language, to have exactly the same properties and relations. This is a version of the principle of the Identity of Indiscernibles. I maintain that the Identity of Indiscernibles, if true at all, is not a necessary truth. But my argument to this effect must be postponed until ch. 9 §1. In the meantime, I simply assert that it is impossible to give an account of the identity of particulars in terms of resemblance. If this is correct, then those who fail to base the symmetry of resemblance upon the symmetry of identity sin against economy of principle.

IV *Can resemblance to paradigms determine properties?*

This is the same difficulty that was brought against Predicate, Concept and Class Nominalism. It was argued that there must be some "ground" in particulars if certain predicates are to apply to them, if they are to fall under certain concepts, if they are to be members of certain classes. But this "ground" – which the Realist will interpret as the objective properties of particulars – is not something of which these theories give any account.

On the Resemblance analysis, a's being F is constituted by a's relations of resemblance to other objects: the paradigms. But, once again, it seems obvious that there must be a "ground" in the object a (not to mention in the paradigm) which determines these relations. It is natural to assert that things resemble because they have something in common, counter-intuitive to say that they have something in common because they resemble each other.[1]

In his *Treatise* (Vol. 1, Bk 1, Part III, § 1) Hume distinguished between "relations of ideas" and "matters of fact". (This is a very important distinction which will be discussed at length in the chapter on Relations in volume II. A more modern terminology is that of "internal" and "external" relations.) Relations of ideas are those where the relation logically depends upon the intrinsic nature of the related things, for example, where one thing is bigger than another. Matters of fact are those where the relation is not logically dependent upon the intrinsic nature of the related things. A case would be that where one thing is distant from another. Now Hume simply takes it as obvious, not requiring discussion, that resemblance is a "relation of ideas". But if so, resemblance is based upon nature, not nature upon resemblance.

One way of bringing out the force of the parallel arguments in the case of Predicate, Concept and Class Nominalism is to conduct the

[1] This point is made by Mackie (1976), ch. 4 § VIII.

thought-experiment of removing the predicate 'F', the concept *F* or the remainder of the class of Fs. It seems clear in each case that *a* might still be F. In the same way, we might make the thought-experiment of removing the paradigm or paradigms which *a* resembles. Surely this leaves *a*'s nature unaffected? However, since in this form the argument raises some important complications, it will be further discussed in the next section.

v *The possible non-existence of paradigms*

Duncan-Jones (1934) asserts:

It is obviously logically possible for only one object in the world to be white. (p. 85)

If this is granted, then what makes a white thing white cannot be its relations of resemblance to other white things. An appeal to hypothetical propositions or to merely possible paradigms seems hopeless. The whole point about paradigms in the Resemblance analysis is that they should be actual objects which can work upon a classifier's mind and so enable him to compare other things with the paradigm.

However, Duncan-Jones' point is somewhat harder to sustain than may appear at first sight. It requires to be supported by some argument. For an ordinary white object will have parts, each of which is a smaller white object, and phases, each of which is a shorter-lived white object. So "a white object" is equally "many white objects". (Contrariwise, as is familiar, the totality of white things can be regarded as forming a single, scattered, perhaps infinite, white object.) It might be argued on Duncan-Jones' behalf that ordinary white things are analysable in terms of point-instant white things which have no parts or phases. But such an analysis is extremely controversial.

It may be possible to find properties where the difficulty just raised about whiteness does not arise. Consider, for instance, the "space-time worm" which is a man's life. One could select some characteristic of this four-dimensional structure (the characteristic might involve a certain size, a certain duration, etc.) and so obtain a particular with a putative property, P, which could not be subdivided into a number of particulars each with the property, P. (The putative property would have at least one mark of a genuine property: it would be *possible* for there to be other, numerically distinct, particulars which were instances of P.) But, against this, it may be plausibly argued that all such properties are analysable in terms of sub-properties where it is not possible to say unambiguously that we have just one instance of the sub-property. Hence, perhaps, an account of P can be given in terms of the sub-properties, and then these sub-properties can be analysed in terms of resemblances.

The question just raised is tangled and difficult. But I think that the argument against the Resemblance analysis can be developed without coming to a decision about the points raised in the previous paragraph. Consider again an ordinary white object, and suppose it to be the only white object in the universe. What account of its whiteness can a Resemblance analysis give? If we ignore solutions in terms of hypothetical truths or merely possible white objects, only two accounts seem available. (a) The proper spatial parts and temporal phases of the white thing are white, these resemble each other, and the whiteness of the whole thing is dependent upon the resemblance of these parts and phases. (b) The white thing as a whole resembles its parts and phases.

If the Resemblance theorist chooses account (a), then the question may be renewed about each proper part or phase. Each of these, it seems, might have been the only white thing in the world, without making any difference to the part's or phase's whiteness. So the whiteness of each part and phase must depend upon the resemblance-relation of sub-parts and sub-phases. If the process does not go to infinity, then ultimate white "atoms" must be reached whose whiteness does not depend in any way upon resemblance. But even if the process does go to infinity, we still never reach anything whose whiteness is genuinely dependent upon *its* resemblance to some further white particular. This falsifies the Resemblance theory.

Suppose, instead, that the Resemblance theorist says that the original white thing, as a whole, resembles its proper parts and/or phases. This suggestion can be taken in two ways. The Resemblance theorist may be relying on the resemblance of the white thing to the collection of its parts (phases). Alternatively, he may have in mind the resemblance of the white thing to individual parts (phases). I consider the alternatives in turn. The difficulty with the first suggestion is that the relation of a whole to its parts is that of *identity*. A whole is the sum of its parts. So the suggestion amounts to saying that a thing resembles itself. Now it seems to me that it is impossible for a thing to resemble itself. (In ch. 19 I shall criticize the notion of reflexive relation.) But even if this point is not pressed and we allow the notion of a thing resembling itself, this certainly cannot be the relation which Resemblance theorists had in mind when they proposed their analysis. If a thing's whiteness is determined by its resemblance to itself, then the appeal to *other* things of the same sort is quite unnecessary. For if this convenient relation of self-resemblance can be appealed to in cases where there is no external thing to resemble, why not appeal to it in all cases of resemblance? This appears to be a *reductio ad absurdum* of the Resemblance analysis.

The alternative is to say that the whole thing as a whole resembles its parts individually. This only postpones the problem. Let the whole thing be *a*, and the proper part it resembles be *b*. If it is *a* less *b* which is said to resemble *b*, then we are back with an account of the whiteness of the white thing in terms of the resemblance of proper parts and phases, an account we have already claimed to refute. If it is *a* including *b* which resembles *b*, then reliance is once again being placed upon the resemblance of *b* to itself.

I conclude, then, that the Resemblance analysis is vulnerable to the criticism that a thing could have a certain property even though there were no other things with that property, a possibility which rules out an analysis of properties in terms of resemblance-relations to paradigms.

VI *Resemblance Nominalism and two infinite regresses*

We saw that Predicate and Concept Nominalism are involved in two vicious regresses: the Object and the Relation regress. In the case of Class Nominalism, only the Relation regress is vicious. In the case of Resemblance Nominalism, the situation is the same as that for Class Nominalism.

It is clear that an Object regress at least threatens a Resemblance analysis. *a* is F if and only if it sufficiently resembles one or more paradigm objects. But what of the paradigms? They must certainly be Fs. If the paradigms for Fs are not Fs, then what will be F? Yet what account can the Resemblance theorist give of their being F? For the reasons given in the previous section, I do not think that he can solve the problem by appealing to the resemblance of the paradigms to themselves. So, given the Resemblance analysis, another paradigm is required for the paradigm to resemble, and an apparently vicious regress begins.

But it seems that the regress can be stopped in the following way. The first set of paradigms must be provided with a second set of paradigms, but after that, it seems, the regress can come round on its own tail. The first set of paradigms are all Fs in virtue of their resemblance to a second set of paradigms. But then it can be said that the second set are all Fs in virtue of their resemblance to the first set.

The position is this. We start with a finite set of sets of particulars, made up, for example, of two of Price's paradigm sets. The *nature*, the F-ness, of each member of one sub-set is determined by its resemblance to each member of the *other* sub-set. The F-ness of *other* Fs is then given by their resemblance to the members of the paradigm sets. The only disadvantage I can see in this is that it makes the F-ness of members of the paradigm set somewhat different from the F-ness of other Fs. But perhaps even this can be accepted. Paradigm Fs are Fs in a somewhat special sense. No doubt the standard metre is a metre long. But it is in a special position among the class of metre-long particulars.

I conclude that the Resemblance analysis survives the Object regress.

The Relation regress is a different matter. Unlike the Relation regress in the case of Predicate, Concept and Class Nominalism, this regress is very well-known. The reason for this is that the argument was presented with the greatest clarity in Russell's *The Problems of Philosophy* (1912).[1] Russell wrote:

> If we wish to avoid the universals *whiteness* and *triangularity*, we shall choose some particular patch of white or some particular triangle, and say that anything is white or a triangle if it has the right sort of resemblance to our chosen particular. But then the resemblance required will have to be a universal. Since there are many white things, the resemblance must hold between many pairs of particular white things; and this is the characteristic of a universal. It will be useless to say that there is a different resemblance to each pair, for then we will have to say that these resemblances resemble each other, and thus at last we shall be forced to

[1] There is an unsatisfactory anticipation of the argument in Mill's *Logic*, Bk II, ch. 2 § III, final note. Husserl, in his *Logical Investigations* (1913) noted the passage in Mill and himself formulated the regress. See Vol. II, Investigation II, ch. 1 §§ 4 and 5.

admit resemblance as a universal. The relation of resemblance therefore, must be a true universal and having been forced to admit this universal, we find that it is no longer worthwhile to invent difficult and implausible theories to avoid the admission of such universals as whiteness and triangularity. (pp. 150–1)

I think that Russell's argument is sound. But many philosophers have contended that the argument fails (for instance, Price, 1953, pp. 23–6). They have denied Russell's assertion that "we shall be forced to admit resemblance as a universal". They reason in the following way. We start with a class of things, such as the class of white things, each member of which is said "to have the same property". This feature of the class is then explained in terms of the relation of resemblance holding between each member of the class and a paradigm. Russell then makes the point that these instances of the relation are all different instances of the same *type* of situation: a resemblance-situation. This is something that even the Nominalist must admit (see the beginning of ch. 2 § iv). How, he asks, are we to account for the unity of this new class, the class of resemblance-situations, without admitting a (relational) universal? But, it is suggested against Russell at this point, these resemblance-situations do not involve something identical. Instead, they simply *resemble* each other. More strictly, it should be said, all these resemblance-situations suitably resemble *a paradigm resemblance-situation*. This creates second-order resemblance-situations and it is conceded that Russell can raise his problem again about them. But these situations can be unified in turn by third-order resemblance-situations. And so *ad infinitum*, but in a virtuous regress.

As in the case of Predicate Nominalism, I do not think that this reply succeeds. The original type, the property of *whiteness* is got rid of, but at the cost of installing another type, the relation of resemblance. Any attempt to get rid of the latter installs another type, a higher-order relation of resemblance (or perhaps further instances of the original relation). At each stage, therefore, the right-hand side of the analysis involves an unanalysed *type*. This type raises the same problem for the Resemblance Nominalist as did the original type.

Suppose, however, what I do not concede, that the infinite regress of resemblance is not a vicious one. Even so, the Resemblance Nominalist pays a great price in answering Russell. The

Resemblance theory is forced to postulate, as part of the furniture of the world, an infinite hierarchy of resemblance-relations. By contrast, the Realist need postulate nothing more than the possession of properties by the resembling objects. So even if the regress were not logically vicious it would be economically vicious.

It may be retorted here that the Realist is as much saddled with a hierarchy of resemblances as the Resemblance theorist. For whatever our solution to the Problem of Universals, where there are at least three objects which "have a common property", then the objects resemble each other in that respect, the three resemblance-situations resemble each other, and so *ad infinitum*. Both theories are therefore committed to the same ontological extravagance. Hence this extravagance cannot be used by the Realist as a reason for preferring the Realist analysis to the Resemblance analysis.

But there is in fact an important difference between the situation of the Realist and that of the Resemblance Nominalist. The Realist will admit that it is possible in the envisaged situation to manufacture a series of ever more complex resemblance-sentences each of which expresses a true proposition. *But he is not compelled to say that a series of different situations correspond to these sentences.* For he can claim that all the sentences express the very same proposition. Compare the truth regress. If p is true, it follows that it is true that p is true, that it is true that it is true that p is true, and so *ad infinitum*. The expanded sentences express true propositions. But they fail to express any more than what was expressed by saying that p is true. So the Realist can agree that the regress of resemblance-sentences do express true propositions, but claim that the sentences fail to express anything more than the original attribution of a common property.

But the Resemblance theorist is in a different and unhappier position. For him the $n+1^{th}$ level of resemblances has to be postulated in order to explain what needs explaining: the unity of the set of resemblances at the nth level. You cannot explain a thing by itself. And so he is ontologically committed to an infinity of resemblance-relations in a way that the Realist is not.

VII *Resemblance Nominalism and causality*

Finally, the Resemblance analysis faces the usual difficulty concerning causality. Given boundary-conditions of a certain sort, object a operates to produce a certain sort of result. This occurs because a

has certain properties. Now it does seem obvious that *a* produces this result because of what *a* itself is. But, given the Resemblance analysis, *a*'s properties are not determined by what *a* itself is but by its relation of resemblance to certain paradigms.

Despite the many difficulties which can be raised against Resemblance Nominalism it is by far the most satisfactory version of Nominalism. The most important insight which it captures is this. Most classes of particulars which are said to be of the same sort, kind or type are not said to be so in virtue of their being *identical* in some way. For the most part, at least, our sortings and classifyings are much looser than this. As Wittgenstein perceived in the case of games, the unity involved is no more than a loose unity of variegated resemblances. In many cases at least, this may take the form of a "sufficient degree of resemblance" to each member of a set of paradigms.

But, against the Resemblance Nominalist, I maintain that such paradigms are types, not tokens, and that universals are required to explain types. Furthermore, I maintain, resemblance can only be analysed in terms of respects of resemblance. Respects, in their turn, require to be explained by means of universals.

6

Arguments for Realism

In the endeavour to avoid admitting objective properties and relations, Nominalists have appealed to predicates, concepts, classes, aggregates and resemblances. In the last four chapters it has been argued that none of these appeals succeeds. However, our examination of Nominalism is not yet completely finished. We have still to consider the Particularist doctrine that there are objective properties and relations, but that these are not universals but particulars, as particular as the objects which have them. For although Particularism can be, and has been, combined with the admission of universal properties and relations, it can also be developed as a form of Nominalism. Particularism will be examined in ch. 8. In the meanwhile, I turn to consider certain positive arguments for Realism. I base myself almost entirely upon a remarkable article by Arthur Pap (1959), together with improvements on Pap's arguments worked out by Frank Jackson (1977).

I *Two statements about colours*

Consider the statements:

(1) Red resembles orange more than it resembles blue.
(2) Red is a colour.

It would generally be granted that both the statements are true. Yet they appear to involve reference to universals. Notice that they could be rewritten with only a surface clumsiness as:

(1′) Redness resembles orangeness more than it resembles blueness.
(2′) Redness is a colour.

It seems that the Nominalist owes the Realist an analysis of the statements from which this ostensible reference to universals has been removed.

Let us begin by considering (1). The Nominalist may suggest that it be rewritten as:

(1″) For all particulars, x, y and z, if x is red and y is orange and z is blue, then x resembles y more than x resembles z .

This is not a Nominalist analysis, but at least ostensible reference to *red(ness)*, *orange(ness)* and *blue(ness)* has been removed. Instead the predicates 'red', 'orange' and 'blue' have been used. The statement is neutral between Nominalism and Realism.

However, as Pap points out, the proposed translation is not equivalent to the original statement. The xs, ys and zs are ordinary particulars and so will have many other characteristics besides colour. Consider, then, the case where x is a red pen, z is a blue pen of identical make, and y is a marigold. In this case x resembles z more closely that x resembles y. So the proposed translation is a false proposition while the original proposition is true. It cannot therefore be a satisfactory translation.

It should be noted, however, that Pap's objection would be met if we accept the Particularist view that the properties of particulars are themselves particular. The variables 'x', 'y' and 'z' can then be taken to range over the particular rednesses, orangenesses and bluenesses of particulars. So interpreted, (1″) appears to express a true proposition. The case against the Nominalist who is also a Particularist about properties and relations must therefore depend upon other objections (see ch. 8).

Given that (1″) fails, it seems that the Nominalist must instead try:

(1‴) For all particulars, x, y and z, if x is red and y is orange and z is blue, then x *colour-resembles* y more than x *colour-resembles* z.

The predicate 'colour-resemblance' here cannot, of course, be analysed as 'resemblance in respect of colour'. Such an analysis would set up a four-term relation of resemblance holding between x, y, z and *colour*. But apparent reference to a universal, *colour*, would have been introduced in place of apparent reference to *redness*, *orangeness* and *blueness*. Rather, the Nominalist must claim, 'colour-resemblance' is a primitive predicate.

But is it a primitive predicate? Donald Davidson (1965) has

taught us to be very suspicious of the claim that such made-up predicates are really primitive. He directs his criticism against the claim that such predicates as 'believes-that-the-cat-is-on-the-mat' could be primitive. He points out that we know how to manufacture, and use understandingly, an indefinite multiplicity of further predicates of this sort, yet it cannot be supposed that we have an indefinite stock of primitive predicates at our disposal.

In the case of predicates having the form 'believes that . . .' we have the whole resources of our language available for making up new predicates. The cases which we are considering do not yield the same easy wealth of predicates. Nevertheless, it is clear that the predicate 'colour-resembles' does not stand on its own. Certain shapes, smells, temperatures, etc. resemble in the same sort of way that our three colours resemble. Each case will demand its own resemblance-predicate. It is a very implausible claim that each of these is a new primitive predicate. It is clear that we understand the pattern which is common to all these predicates and that it is this understanding which permits us to form new resemblance-predicates as required. What is common can only be resemblance and what is peculiar to each case can only be the *respect* of the resemblance.

Frank Jackson has strengthened this general consideration by further particular arguments. I refer readers to his article (1977).

I turn now to our second proposition:

(2) Red is a colour.

It seems that the Nominalist has even less room for manœuvre here than in the case of (1). He must attempt to translate (2) as:

(2′) For all particulars, x, if x is red, then x is coloured.

It is clear that (2) entails (2′), but the question is whether the reverse entailment holds. Jackson has a simple and beautiful argument to show that it does not. Consider:

(3′) For all particulars, x, if x is red, then x is extended.

(3′) is true. Indeed, like (2′), it appears to be a necessary truth. (If the case of visual points is thought to falsify (3′) then 'extended' may be taken in the minimal sense of 'spatial'.) Hence, by parity, if (2′) entails (2), then (3′) should entail:

(3) Red(ness) is an extension.

So far from this being the case, however, (3) is actually *false*. It follows that (2) says more than (2'). The Nominalist has given no account of this.

It is to be noted once again that this argument fails against a Particularist view of properties. The Particularist can analyse (2) as:

> (2″) For all (ordinary) particulars, x, if x has a (particular) red-ness, then x has a (particular) colouredness *and* the class of the particular rednesses is a sub-class of the class of the particular colourednesses.

By contrast, he will analyse (3') as:

> (3″) For all (ordinary) particulars, x, if x has a (particular) red-ness, then x has a (particular) extendedness *and it is not the case that* the class of the particular rednesses is a sub-class of the class of the particular extendednesses.

The Particularist will still require an account of the second conjunct of (2″). But this seems to give him no especial problem. He could, for instance, make the particular colourednesses second-order (though particularized) properties: properties of the particular rednesses.

We see, then, that the arguments of this section, though very powerful against orthodox Nominalism, fail against Nominalism when it is combined with Particularism. In another way, also, it is important not to overestimate the arguments. They show, I think, that no Nominalist account is possible of certain (obviously true) statements about colours. By implication, the same holds for various statements about other ranges of qualities. But the arguments do not prove that, for instance, there is such a property as *redness* or a property, *being coloured*. At a much later stage (ch. 22 § 1) I shall in fact be arguing that there are no such properties. The determinate shades of red and the other colours are properties, but the determin-ables, *redness* and *colour*, are mere classes of properties. As a result, the correct positive analysis of our two statements is by no means straightforward. All the argument of the present section seems to show is that Nominalists who are not Particularists cannot deal with the statements.

II *Attribute variables*

Pap also raises the question what account the Nominalist can give of statements like 'He has the same virtues as his father' and 'The dresses were of the same colour'. A natural way to render the former, for instance, is:

> For all properties, F, if F is a virtue, then a has F if and only if a's father has F.

This is unacceptable to the Nominalist, of course, because it mentions properties. What alternative analysis can he offer?

A *Predicate* Nominalist might suggest:

> For all particulars, x, if x is a virtue-predicate, then x applies to a if and only if x applies to a's father.

As Pap points out in connection with a different example, this translation will be adequate only if there are virtue-predicate tokens corresponding to *each* virtue, and it is not a necessary truth that this is the case. This difficulty can be obviated by letting *x* range over all *possible* particulars, but only at the cost of committing the Predicate Nominalist to *possibilia*. However, the most serious difficulty concerns the predicate 'virtue-predicate'. It is clear that the predicate cannot be a primitive one: conditions for its application must be given. What can those conditions be except that it applies to any predicate which in turn applies to any particular which possesses one of the virtues? But to speak of 'one of the virtues' is to make ostensible reference to universals.

The same sort of difficulty will arise for:

> For all classes, x, if x is a virtue-class [that is, a class of persons each having a certain virtue], then a is a member of x if and only if a's father is a member of x.

or for:

> For all particulars, x, if x is a virtue-paradigm [that is, a paradigm of a certain virtue], then a suitably resembles x if and only if a's father suitably resembles x.

At the end of § 1, I said that I did not think that Pap's argument showed that there is such a property as *being red* or *being coloured*. In

the same way, I do not think that the argument from attribute
variables shows that the virtues must be genuine properties. An *a
posteriori* Realism cannot be content to establish the existence of
particular universals as easily as that! But I think that the argument
does show that we can give an account of 'the virtues' only in terms
of universals: that range of properties and relations which make it
true that a particular possesses a certain virtue.

7

Transcendent Universals

1 *The nature of the theory*

We turn now to a version of Realism. It resembles the four Nominalist analyses already considered in being a *Relational* theory. According to this view, *a* has the property, F, if and only if *a* has a suitable relation to the transcendent universal or Form of F. Traditionally, the view is ascribed to Plato. It was revived by Moore and Russell at the beginning of this century.

It will be convenient to speak of transcendent universals as Forms. But it is important to realise that Plato's theory of Forms is a theory which claims to do more than simply solve the problem of universals. The problem of universals is the problem how different particulars can nevertheless have the very same properties and relations. It is the problem of generic identity. The Platonic theory of Forms is intended to solve this problem. But it is intended to do more besides.

First, there is the problem of *uninstantiated properties* such as (perhaps) *travelling faster than light*, or even Hume's missing shade of blue. Postulating transcendent Forms might be thought to provide for the existence of such properties.

This problem is rather a peculiar one. Why should we think it is necessary to provide for the existence of such properties? Why not simply say that there are no such things? It must be admitted that there is a predicate 'travels faster than light'. But why, unless the predicate applies to something, allow that there is a property of travelling faster than light?

It may be thought that the theory of meaning requires such a property. The predicate 'travels faster than light' is a perfectly good predicate. The expression means something. The corresponding property must therefore exist to be what is meant.

This argument takes meaning to be a dyadic relation holding between expressions and what is meant, and it is now widely appreciated that this is a crude and unsatisfactory theory of meaning. What is much more difficult is to provide a satisfactory substitute. That problem, however, is a problem for semantic theory, and I will make no attempt to solve it here. There is a long but, I think, on the whole discreditable tradition which tries to settle ontological questions on the basis of semantic considerations.

It is not clear to what extent this argument from meaning was one that moved Plato himself. In the *Republic* Socrates says:

> shall we proceed as usual and begin by assuming the existence of a single essential nature or Form for every set of things which we call by the same name? (595)

But is Plato arguing here that the Form is required for the name to be meaningful? That is the way in which he is often interpreted. However, it is at least as plausible to suggest that the underlying argument is that sameness of name requires sameness of nature in the things named. The argument is then a version (admittedly a linguistic version and therefore in my view an unsatisfactory version) of the One over Many argument.

Second, Forms are postulated to solve a particular problem about uninstantiated properties: the problem of ideal limits. Thus, Plato and others argue that no ordinary object is ever perfectly circular, and no human act ever perfectly good. Again, Newtonian physics makes assertions about what happens to bodies which are not acted upon by any forces at all, although it also asserts that there are no such bodies. Forms may then be postulated to be the ideal limits to which mere particulars can only approximate. Among other things, they can then function as objective ethical standards.

Once again, however, there seems to be no need to do more than postulate the corresponding predicates or concepts. Ideal limits are conceptual devices used to classify actual instances by reference to the degree of divergence that there would be between the actual and the ideal instances if the latter were to exist. The hypothetical propositions involved do not seem to raise any particular ontological problems. It is the actual instances, and these alone, which make the hypothetical propositions true.

Third, Forms may act as the referents for apparent referring expressions in mathematical, logical and other statements. For instance, we talk about the number four and its properties. This may suggest that the number four, although not an ordinary particular, is an object in its own right. I think that this is the most weighty argument for transcendent Forms, but I will not consider it further here. A brief account of number will be given in ch. 18 § v.

II *What relation holds between particulars and Forms?*

With the possible exception of classes, the entities to which the Nominalist analyses appeal (unsuccessfully, I have argued) are not postulated entities. There are such things as predicates and concepts, and these apply or fail to apply to particulars. There are such things as paradigm instances and there are other particulars which resemble the paradigms more or less closely. And even in the case of classes, there is a clear sense in which there are classes, and particulars which are members of these classes.

Transcendent Forms are quite different. They are theoretical entities, standing apart from the ordinary world, postulated in the same general sort of way that atoms or genes were postulated, to explain certain phenomena. In a matter of fundamental ontology, this is a *prima facie*, although certainly no more than a *prima facie*, disadvantage of the theory of Forms.

Not only are Forms postulated entities, but so is the relation between particular and Form which bestows a nature upon the particular. Just what is the nature of this relation? This has always been a puzzle for upholders of the theory. In Plato's *Parmenides* the young Socrates first suggests that the relation is that of *participation* and then that it is *imitation*.

If "participation" is understood literally, then each particular simply gets a numerically different part of the Form. This is clearly unsatisfactory. The problem is to explain how different particulars can all have something in common. But if the Form has to be broken up among the particulars, then the problem of what is common to the particulars is replaced by the problem by what criterion these parts of the Form are all accounted parts of the same thing. Which is no advance at all. But if the word "participation" is not to be taken literally, what is the relation which is meant?

Imitation involves another set of problems. The asymmetrical relation of imitation entails, but is not entailed by, the symmetrical relation of resemblance. What condition must be added to the condition that *a* resembles *b* to yield the conclusion that *a* imitates *b*? Presumably we are not interested here in that perhaps primary sense of "imitate" which involves the existence of agents with purposes. White things do not imitate the Form of whiteness in that sense.

An instance of the sense required seems to be that where a chameleon imitates or, as we also say, "takes on" the colour of its environment. We might call it "natural" imitation. It is clear that a causal relation is involved here. The environment acts upon the chameleon, acting in virtue of a certain property: the predominant colour of the environment. The result is that the chameleon comes to have the same property. It might be objected to this account of imitation that it has the consequence that when the heat of the fire makes the water hot, the water imitates the fire. However, the consequence may not be as objectionable as it seems at first hearing. We would be prepared to say that the water takes on (some of) the heat of the fire. But, in any case, the situation with the chameleon is more causally sophisticated, requiring a universal quantification over properties for its statement. The chameleon "imitates" the environment because whatever predominant colour its environment assumes, as a result the chameleon takes on just that colour.

This analysis of "natural" imitation makes it clear, however, that the notion presupposes, and so cannot be used to explain, the notion of "the same property". That such imitation involves causal action is a further stumbling-block. At one time Plato thought of the Forms as causes of events and states of affairs in the world of particulars (*Phaedo*, 95–106). But I do not think that any contemporary believer in transcendent universals would follow him here. So it seems that this sense of "imitation" cannot be the sense appropriate to the theory of Forms. But what is the appropriate sense?

It is interesting, but somewhat saddening, to notice that the great modern defenders of transcendent universals, Moore and Russell, do not even consider this problem of the nature of the relation between particulars and Forms to which Plato gave such close attention. But for those who do face the problem it seems that the best thing to do (*faute de mieux*) is to assert that the relation in question is completely indefinable, but that its nature is grasped, unreflectively at least, by everybody who understands what it is for things to have properties and relations. Cook Wilson (1926, § 148) took this view and wrote:

In fact the relation of the universal to the particular is something *sui generis*, presupposed in any explanation of anything. The nature of the universal therefore necessarily and perpetually eludes any attempt to explain itself. The recognition of this enables one to elucidate the whole puzzle of the *Parmenides* of Plato. (p. 348)

III *Can Forms determine properties?*

The difficulty to be discussed in this section is the same as that brought against the varieties of Nominalism. Is it not clear that *a*'s whiteness is not determined by *a*'s relationship with a transcendent entity? Perform the usual thought-experiment and consider *a* without the Form of Whiteness. It seems obvious that *a* might still be white. So *a*'s being white is not determined by *a*'s relation to the Form.

It is important to see that this argument succeeds only against a doctrine of *transcendent* universals. It would fail against the view that "participation" meant that a proper part of the Form was actually in *a*. It would also fail against the view that the Form is something *present as a whole* in *a* (as well as present as a whole in other particulars). The first of these alternatives is worthless, because it breaks up the unity of the Form. The second alternative, however, must be taken very seriously. It will be examined in ch. 10. It comes close to what I take to be the truth of the matter.

It may be thought that the parallel with the difficulty urged against the varieties of Nominalism breaks down here for another reason. It may be said that the relations between predicates, concepts, classes and paradigms, on the one hand, and suitable particulars, on the other, are not *productive* relations. They do nothing to make the particulars what they are. Hence they cannot serve to give an account of what it is for particulars to have properties and relations. But the Form can be thought of as productive. When the Form comes to have the converse of participation to an object, then that object takes on a certain character.

The half-expressed thought behind the word "productive" is that the relation is a species of causal relation. (Unless, indeed, it is that the Form is actually present in the particular.) But the causal relation demands a cause and an effect, each having their own properties. So it cannot be used to give an account of what it is to have a property. What seems needed is that the Form's relation to the object be not simply productive but also *logically constitutive*. *a*'s whiteness is constituted by, is nothing but, the relation in which Form and object stand. But once the distinction between productive and constitutive relations is clearly grasped, then either the view being defended turns into an *immanent* view, or else any appearance of difference between the relation of Form to object and the relations of predicate, concept, class, aggregate or paradigm to object disappears. Suppose that *a* and *b* have quite different properties. According to the theory of transcendent Forms they are *in themselves* exactly the same. Their only differences lie in their relational properties: their relations to a different set of Forms. But may there not be a difference of nature in *a* and *b*, beyond mere numerical difference? Yet this difference the theory of Forms could not account for.

A perception of this difficulty may be one reason why, in the Platonic version of the theory, particulars are regularly presented as less real than the Forms. In Plato's philosophy, particulars are, as it were, in danger of being swallowed up by the Forms. In *The Problems of Philosophy* (1912) Russell proclaims the equal reality of the realm of particulars and the realm of Forms and says that Plato's view is unphilosophical. Russell says that the philosopher should take an egalitarian attitude to every entity which he admits into his ontology. But there are real *intellectual* pressures behind the Platonic position, pressures of which Russell is insufficiently aware. Once particulars are admitted to be as real as the Forms, the case for their properties being the particulars' own, and not simply constituted by the particulars' relation to external Forms, is enormously strengthened.

IV *The Forms and two infinite regresses*

It will be argued in this section that the theory of Forms, if it is taken to be a theory of universals, resembles Class and Resemblance Nominalism in that an Object regress does not, but a Relation regress does, obtain.

Predicate Nominalism analyses *a*'s being F in terms of the applicability of 'F' to *a*. But the predicate 'F' is something repeatable: it is a type. Hence the Object regress is born. Class Nominalism analyses *a*'s being F in terms of *a*'s membership of the class of Fs. The class of Fs is not a type: there can only be one class of all the Fs. So in this case the Object regress fails. What of the Form of F? It seems clear that in this respect it resembles the class rather than the predicate. The Form of F is necessarily unique. Hence no One over Many problem arises in connection with it.

I take this to be the point of Plato's *Third Bed* argument (*Republic*, 597), if indeed it is really meant to be an argument. Plato says that there can only be one Form of the Bed. For, if there were two, a third Bed must appear above the two, and this would be the Bed. Commentators have puzzled about the suppressed premisses of this argument. But is it best taken as an argument? I think Plato (whatever he thinks he is doing) should simply be taken to be emphasizing the *essential uniqueness* of the Form.

So the Object regress fails against the Forms. But there is a price to be paid. What is brought out in rebutting the Object regress is the extent to which the unrepeatable Forms are simply strange or metaphysical particulars. Extremes have a habit of meeting, in philosophy as elsewhere, and the Nominalist can quite plausibly claim that Forms do not violate the rule that 'all things that exist are only particulars'.[1] If so, it will not be surprising that the same sorts of difficulties which hold for Nominalism also hold for the theory of Forms.

By contrast, the Relation regress, first stated, as far as I know, by Ryle (1939, pp. 137–8), appears to be vicious. Particulars participate in Forms. The relation of *participation* is therefore a type having indefinitely many tokens. But this is the very sort of situation which the theory of Forms finds unintelligible and insists on explaining by means of a Form. The theory is therefore committed to setting up a Form of Participation in which ordered pairs consisting of a particular and a first-order Form *participate*.

Once again, however, the problem is reproduced. If this second-order participation is something different in nature from first-order participation, then it requires to be explained by third-order participation, and so *ad infinitum*. But if second-order participation is the same in nature as first-order participation, then the analysis of first-order participation is proceeding in terms of this (first-order) participation in a Form, which is circular.

It appears, then, that the Relation regress holds against *all* Relational analyses of what it is for an object to have a property or relation. If a's being F is analysed as a's having R to a ø, then Raø is one of the situations of the sort that the theory undertakes to

[1] A point argued for and emphasized by Donald Brownstein (1973).

analyse. So it must be a matter of the ordered pair $< a,\emptyset >$ having R' to a new ø-like entity: $\emptyset_R$. If R and R' are different, the same problem arises with R' and so *ad infinitum*. If R and R' are identical, then the projected analysis of Raø has appealed to R itself, which is circular.

v *The Third Man*

The Object and the Relation regresses are distinct from the more famous regress known as the Third Man. The Third Man is an unsound argument. But it is worth examination, if only to see clearly how it differs from the other two regresses.

The argument, presented in the *Parmenides*, is that if we consider the particulars which 'have a certain property' *plus* the Form which explains the possession of the property, we see that particulars and Form constitute a new *many* which demands a new or second-order Form to be their *one*. But this new Form gives rise to yet a further *many*, demanding yet another *one*, and so *ad infinitum*. The one Form becomes many Forms.

It is now generally appreciated that the argument depends upon a premiss, the Self-predication assumption, that the Form which accounts for particulars having a certain property, itself has that property. The Form of Whiteness, say, is itself something white. Only if this is true can the argument advance.

But why should we grant that the Form of F is an F? What we encounter here is the topic of *higher-order universals*: properties and relations *of* properties and relations. This difficult topic must await a much later stage in the argument (Part Seven). But we can see now that, in general at least, F-ness is not an F. *Whiteness* is a colour (one of the colours), but there seems no reason to say that *whiteness* is coloured. If *whiteness* is not coloured, it is not white. And if *whiteness* is not white, why should we say that the Form of white is white? With the denial of Self-predication, the Third Man collapses.

It must, of course, be conceded that the Third Man is effective *ad hominem* against Plato. For Plato did think, or tend to think, of the Forms not simply as transcendent universals but also as paradigms which the particulars that fell under them resembled. His theory was, in part, a transcendent version of Resemblance Nominalism. Hence the Third Man has an abiding interest for investigations of Plato's thought. It is, nevertheless, a mistake to treat transcendent universals as celestial paradigms. There is no need for a modern defender of the Forms to follow Plato in this.

Here it is interesting to notice what happens if we try to construct a parallel version of the Third Man in the case of the other Relational analyses. The predicate 'F' is generally not an F. Few tokens of 'white' are white. It is therefore not possible to construct the Third Man argument against Predicate Nominalism. In the same way, the concept *F* is not in general an F. Could it be urged against the Class analysis, that in the case of apparently unstructured properties such as *whiteness*, the class of white things is itself white, and hence that a more inclusive class is required? The Class Nominalist will reply by distinguishing between aggregates and classes. He will agree that the aggregate of white things is white, but deny that the class is white. (If he does not make this distinction, his theory collapses into Mereological Nominalism.) So here, too, it seems that the Third Man fails.

Only in the case of the Resemblance analysis can the argument get off the ground, because paradigm Fs *are* Fs. For this special case, however, the Third Man is only minimally different from the Object regress. The Object regress when deployed against the Resemblance theory asks what account the latter can give of the F-ness of paradigm Fs. The Third Man takes the class consisting of ordinary Fs plus the paradigms, and then asks what account is to be given of the common nature of the members of the class. But as argued in ch. 5 § VI, the answer to both difficulties can be the same. We set up at least two classes of paradigm Fs, where the members of one class act as paradigms for each of the members of the other. The rest of the class of Fs suitably resemble these paradigm Fs. In this way, there is no need to go outside the class of Fs to a 'third F'.

So the Third Man is ineffective not simply against the theory of Forms, but also against the other Relational analyses of what it is for something to have a property.

VI *The Restricted Third Man*

Nevertheless, there does seem to be a *special case* of the Third Man which creates some difficulty for a theory of transcendent universals. We may call it the "Restricted Third Man".

Consider the Forms. Each of them is its own unique self. But they do have something in common. They are different tokens of the one type. They are all Forms. Formhood is a one which runs through this many. So must there not be a Form of Formhood? By participating in this Form, the lower-order Forms gain the character of Forms. If the supporter of Forms does not acquiesce in this reasoning, he has the difficult task of explaining why he holds that the same reasoning is valid in the case of ordinary particulars which have a common property.

Now while in general the Form of F is not an F, the Form of Formhood is, of course, a Form. The Self-predication assumption must hold for this special case. The Restricted Third Man regress can now be developed. Consider the collection of first-order Forms plus the Form of Formhood. The members of this expanded collection have something in common. The different tokens are all of the same type. In consistency, therefore, they must all be said to participate in a third-order Form of Formhood. The regress then continues. It is either vicious or, at best, uneconomical.

However, this does not end the argument. The ordinary Third Man does not simply depend upon the Self-predication assumption. It also depends upon a Non-identity assumption: that the higher-order Form is distinct from the original Form. If particular Fs participated in the Form of F, and the Form of F was an F, *but the Form of F participated in itself*, then the "regress" would still be perfectly harmless. Applying this to the Restricted Third Man, it may be suggested that first-order Forms participate in the Form of Formhood but the Form of Formhood participates in itself. The Restricted Third Man then goes no further.

But to deny the Non-identity assumption is, in effect, to take a stand on a certain question in the theory of higher-order universals. It is to maintain that a property can have itself as a property: that there can be states of affairs of the form F(F). The question will be discussed briefly in ch. 23 § 11, following on the rejection in ch. 19 § vi, of states of affairs where a thing is related to itself. It will be argued that a property cannot have itself as one of its properties. If so, then the Restricted Third Man does lead to vicious regress.

Since we are now alerted to the parallelism between the various Relational analyses, we will naturally expect that versions of the Restricted Third Man will cause trouble for the other theories besides the theory of Forms. Our expectation will not be disappointed.

In general, the predicate 'F' is not an F. But consider tokens of the various predicates 'F', 'G', . . . etc. Each of these tokens is a predicate. The Predicate Nominalist must analyse this situation by saying that each token falls under the predicate 'predicate'. Now, unlike ordinary particulars, tokens of the new predicate 'predicate' do fall under the predicate 'predicate'. Consider now the set of first-order predicate-tokens plus the tokens of 'predicate'. The members of this augmented set are all tokens of the same type. The Predicate Nominalist may then try to explain their common character by saying that they all fall under the higher-order predicate 'predicate$_1$', and so on indefinitely. But if the argument of ch. 2 § iv was sound, then this regress is vicious for a Predicate Nominalist.

The regress can be halted if the Non-identity assumption can be challenged. Suppose that tokens of 'F', of 'G', etc. fall under 'predicate', but tokens of 'predicate' fall under themselves. There is no regress.

But paradox then follows. Since 'predicate' falls under itself, there is a predicate 'predicate falling under itself'. Equally, there is a predicate 'predicate not falling under itself' under which most tokens of predicates fall. But tokens of this latter predicate can neither fall under the predicate nor can they not fall under the predicate. The assumption that tokens of 'predicate' fall under themselves is incoherent.

The paradox can be avoided by introducing a hierarchy of predicates: 'predicate falling$_0$ under itself', 'predicate falling$_1$ under itself' and so on, (see Quine, 1966, pp. 9–10). 'Predicate falling$_0$ under itself' cannot fall$_0$ under itself, but may fall under predicates in the hierarchy with higher subscripts. But for the Predicate Nominalist this again involves vicious regress. For his account of what it is to be a token of the type 'predicate falling$_n$ under itself' must be given in terms of the predicate 'predicate falling $_{n+1}$ under itself'.

It is clear that the same difficulties can be created for Concept Nominalism.

Class Nominalism is involved in similar difficulties. The class of Fs will not in general be an F. But consider any class of *classes*. This will be a class. Now pass in review the first-order classes plus the classes of classes. They are all tokens of a common type: each is a class. The Class Nominalist must give an account of this type in terms of membership of a common class. Add this class to the original collection. The process must then be repeated *ad infintumi*.

The alternative is to deny the Non-identity assumption and say that the class-character of this all-inclusive class is explained by saying that it is a member of itself. But if it is allowed that this class is a member of itself, it must equally be allowed that there are other classes which are not members of themselves. The Class Nominalist can only explain their "common nature" by saying that they are all members of the one class. Russell's paradox follows. (Susan Haack has pointed out to me that Cantor's paradox can also be brought against the notion of an all-inclusive class.) Again the Restricted Third Man creates difficulty.

Only in the case of the Resemblance analysis does the Restricted Third Man fail. Or, rather, there is no point in trying to formulate a Restricted Third Man against Resemblance Nominalism. For the object of the restriction was to produce cases where the Self-predication assumption holds. But that assumption holds in all cases for the Resemblance analysis. In ch. 5 § VI however, it was argued that, despite this, no vicious regress is involved.

VII *Transcendent universals and causality*

The usual difficulty can be raised which was raised in connection with the other Relational analyses. It is natural to say both that the causal powers of a particular are determined by its properties, and that these powers are determined by the particular's own self and not by anything beyond it. But if the theory of transcendent universals is accepted, a thing's properties are not determined by its own self, but rather by the relations it has to Forms beyond itself.

VIII *Transcendent versus immanent universals*

Transcendent Realism makes a major error in keeping particulars and universals apart. But, before leaving the topic, we should note that it appears to offer prospects of solving a problem of which traditional versions of *immanent* theories of universals make heavy weather.

In turning away from Nominalism it is all too easy to assume that, wherever tokens are of the same type, then there must be something identical in virtue of which the tokens are of the same type. The Nominalist can then counter-attack, asking to be shown this identity in specific cases. Take the class of human beings. Is there really something which all human beings have in common in virtue of which they are human beings? Consider men, women, children, geniuses, mongols, the decorticated, mutations, quadruple amputees and so on. Is there really a one thing which holds together the many? The same sort of puzzle can be developed for almost any other type one cares to consider. Is there really something common to all red things which makes them red? If two things are exactly the same shade of red, then it is not implausible to think that an identity is involved. But is there anything common to things of a different shade of red? It is not clear that there is.

The Absolute Idealist response to this difficulty was to speak of identity-in-difference. This is as much as to say, identity without identity, which is incoherent. The Absolute Idealists accepted this consequence, drawing the conclusion that there could not be a plurality of things.

Transcendent universals may be seen as another way of reacting to the same problem. If universals stand apart from particulars, then the latter may participate in or imitate the former to a greater or lesser degree. Tokens may be imperfect or eccentric representatives of their type. From this perspective, lack of immanence becomes an advantage.

There is, however, a much simpler solution to the difficulty than the desperate expedients of Absolute Idealism or transcendent universals. It is a solution already hinted at by the Resemblance Nominalist, but barred to him by his Nominalism. The solution consists in taking an immanent view of universals, but denying any *simple* identification of sorts, kinds and types with universals. An account of sorts, kinds and types must be given in terms of universals. It must be given in terms of the properties and/or relations of the tokens said to be all of one type. But the properties and/or relations which make different particulars to be of a certain sort, kind, or type need not be identical in the different particulars. Most of our sortings and classifyings are no more than a first approximation to, or rough stab at, a genuine unifying principle. To break through to genuine identities calls for the profound siftings of the whole scientific enterprise.

Provided, then, that we resist the too simple identification of types with universals, it is possible to continue to uphold an Immanent Realism.

8

Properties and relations as particulars

If our arguments up to this point have been correct, then no "Relational" account of what it is for a thing to have a certain property is correct. The clue to the properties of things must be sought within the things themselves. We must look to some form of the doctrine of *universalia in rebus*.

But before doing this we must consider a very important assumption which we have so far not questioned. It has been tacitly assumed that if we admit that things have objective properties and relations, properties and relations not constituted by the relation of the things to predicate, concept, class, aggregate, paradigm, or Form, then we are accepting a version of Realism. It has been tacitly assumed that objective properties and relations are universals. This view has been contested.

According to G. F. Stout (1921, 1923, 1936), with whom the doctrine is most closely associated in twentieth-century Anglo-Saxon philosophy, if a curtain and a carpet are, as we ordinarily say, "both red", then not only do we have two numerically different things – the curtain and the carpet – but we also have two numerically different *rednesses*. This has nothing to do with the fact that the two objects may be two different shades of red. Let the two objects resemble one another exactly in their shade. According to Stout, there are still two numerically different rednesses. Orthodox Realism would say that the two objects were of the *identical* shade of red: the objects are different but they have the same property. But on Stout's view this is false. Stout need not deny that we can say of the curtain and carpet that they are "the very same shade of red". But this is a piece of ordinary language which must not be interpreted as the Realist would interpret it. Stout applies the doctrine to relations as much as to properties, but, just as in our earlier discussions, it will be convenient, yet will not affect the argument, if we restrict ourselves to properties.

It is important to realize that this "Particularist" view of properties and relations, a term already used in ch. 6, is not just an eccentricity of Stout's. Stout's emphasis upon the point, and the forthright way he stated the doctrine, makes his a "classical" exposition. But at least traces of the doctrine, and perhaps much more, are to be found in Plato, in Aristotle and in the Scholastics.[1]

In more recent times the doctrine has been held explicitly by C. S. Peirce, J. Cook Wilson and H. W. B. Joseph. In a paper "The Elements of Being" (1953) D. C. Williams makes the doctrine the centre of an ambitious and fascinating scheme for a "first philosophy". But more than this, the view is one which exerts a continuous pull – a continuous distorting effect, I believe – upon many philosophers' reasonings about universals. The effect is all the more dangerous where, as is quite often the case, the source of the distortion is not recognized. It is of the greatest value to have the Particularist view of properties explicitly before us.

We should take note of a problem of terminology. The problem is a plethora of riches. Stout calls the particulars which he postulates "abstract particulars" (1923, p. 114). In calling them "abstract" it is not meant that they are other-worldly (a perverse contemporary use of the term "abstract"). Stout, in fact, thinks of them as *the* stuff of the world, being followed in this by D. C. Williams. It is simply that these particulars are "thin" and therefore abstract by comparison with the "thick" or concrete particulars which are constituted out of the abstract particulars. Bergmann speaks of "perfect particulars" (1967, Part 1, § v), Strawson of "particularized qualities" (1959,

---

[1] Demos (1946) presents evidence for a Particularist element in Plato's thought about universals, although Demos himself does not link his findings with Particularism. Indications in Aristotle which appear to betray a leaning towards Particularism are well-known. See, for instance, Jones (1949) and Matthews and Cohen (1968). A leaning towards Particularism in Scholastic thought has not, as far as I know, been carefully documented, although I believe that it could be. In the meantime, however, I offer the following quotation from a contemporary philosopher writing in the Scholastic tradition:

> A distinction must be drawn between the abstract property (e.g. whiteness) and the individual instantiation of the property in a thing (indicated by the predicate 'is-white'). ø-in-a is the latter; it is not identical with ø-in-b. Both of these are individual and concrete. They are the real grounds in a and b which permit me to predicate ø of both objects. These are not things but aspects of different things, and they are not identical. We can speak of *identity* only at the abstract level of meaning. (McMullin, 1958.)

p. 168 n. 1), Matthews and Cohen of "unit properties" (1968), Williams of "tropes" and Wolterstorff of "cases" (1970). The term "property-instances" is often used, among Australian philosophers at least. I should have liked to use Stout's term "abstract particulars". Unfortunately, however, I require that phrase to describe another, subtly different, sort of entity (see ch. 11 § v). I shall therefore, besides calling the doctrine "Particularism", speak in this chapter of "Stoutian" particulars. The term is inelegant, but it may help to reduce the chance of misunderstanding.

A final point. In Part Seven it will be argued that universals can themselves fall under universals, that is to say, that properties and relations themselves can have properties and be related. A universal which falls under a universal is *ipso facto* a particular as well as a universal. It is, however, a *higher-order* particular. But the doctrine of Particularism, the doctrine to be considered in this chapter, is the doctrine that the properties and relations of first-order, or ordinary, particulars are themselves *first-order* particulars.

1 *Arguments for Particularism*

What are the arguments for a Particularist view?

First, there is the problem about the multiple location of a property. Consider the curtain and the carpet again. Suppose now that one but not the other ceases to be red. *Redness* has not ceased to exist. But has not *one redness* ceased to exist? If the *redness* of curtain and carpet is identical, as the orthodox view maintains, then the one entity must be conceived of as being wholly present in a multitude of different places and times. How can this be?

The upholder of the Identity view (as we may in this chapter call the doctrine that properties and relations are universals) will reply to this argument by saying that it begs the question. It treats identity of property as if it were identity of a particular. A particular cannot be wholly present in a multitude of different places and times. But a property can. This is to say no more than: a number of different particulars can all have the very same property.

This reply to the Particularist argument does nothing to refute the Particularist view. But the reply seems to show that the Particularist has done nothing to refute the Identity view either.

Second, there appear to be ways of speaking where the object of reference is not the property of a particular considered as a universal, but, rather, as a particular. 'The dress has startling design.' Here, presumably, we are dealing with a universal. The design may be found in other dresses, and in each case it will be startling. But compare 'His poor physical condition led to his collapse'. It is the poor condition that *he* was in, and not any other poor condition, which led to the specific event of his collapse. Now is not his poor condition a *particularized* property?

How could the Identity theorist reply to this argument? It seems that he must at this point introduce the notion of a situation, or, as we shall say, *a state of affairs*. A state of affairs I define as a particular's having a certain property, or two or more particulars standing in a certain relation. In rejecting Nominalism, I have in effect been arguing that it is impossible to give an account of universality purely in terms of particulars. I shall be arguing shortly (ch. 9) that it is impossible to give an account of particularity purely in terms of universals: a thing is not a mere "bundle of properties". But although universality cannot be reduced to particularity, nor particularity to universality, particulars and universals do not stand in splendid isolation from each other. Particulars are particulars falling under universals and universals demand particulars. We can put this by saying that particulars and universals are found only in states of affairs.

I do not think that the recognition of states of affairs involves introducing a new entity. At any rate, it seems misleading to say that there are particulars, universals *and* states of affairs. For it is of the essence of particulars and universals that they involve, and are only found in, states of affairs. More will have to be said about this in ch. 11.

The introduction of the notion of states of affairs serves, among other things, to rebut the Particularist contention that such statements as 'His poor physical condition led to his collapse' must refer to particularized properties. For the Identity theorist can give an account of the truth-conditions of the statement which is at least as plausible as the Particularist account. The Identity theorist will argue as follows. A certain particular, the man, has a certain property or properties and/or relations which make it true that the man is in a poor condition. (The predicate 'being in poor condition' need not itself apply in virtue of a single property.) This state of affairs, together perhaps with other factors, brings about the man's collapse. We have argued earlier that it is particulars that cause, but that they act as causes in virtue of the properties they have. This appears to be equivalent to treating states of affairs, as we have defined them, as causes.

Once again it is not being argued (here) that the Identity account of 'His poor physical condition led to his collapse' must be pre-ferred to the Particularist analysis. All that is being argued is that we do not have to accept the Particularist analysis.

A third line of argument available to the Particularist is of some subtlety. An ordinary particular, or thing, he may argue, is nothing more than the sum of its properties. To deny this, he may say, is to embrace the untenable doctrine that ordinary particulars involve both properties and a supporting substratum. It is to take what may be called the Lockean view of particulars.[1] At the same time, the Particularist may go on, it is possible for two such particulars to resemble in every way. This second step in the argument is the denial of the principle of the Identity of Indiscernibles. The denial is in some degree controversial but I think it is correct. It will be discussed in detail in ch. 10. Consider, now, two particulars which resemble each other exactly. If the Identity analysis of properties is correct, then the two particulars will have the very same properties. (On the Particularist analysis, they will have numerically different but exactly resembling properties.) But if things are nothing but the sum of their properties, the two things will not be two but one. Which is contrary to what was meaningfully supposed. Hence the Identity analysis of properties cannot be correct.

This third argument may be presented again more briefly thus: The propositions:

(1) A particular is nothing but the sum of its properties
(2) Two particulars can resemble exactly
(3) The Identity view of properties is correct

form an inconsistent triad. Not all three can be true. But (1) and (2) must be accepted. So (3) must be rejected.

This argument is suggested by Stout (1921) but not presented in quite this way. The propositions really do seem to form an incon-sistent triad, yet all three have considerable plausibility. All have been held, if not all together, by various philosophers. Hence

[1] Those who do not believe that this was Locke's view are invited to add sneer-quotes to the word "Lockean" throughout.

consideration of the argument is likely to yield conclusions of some interest. But, I believe, the correct reaction to the argument is to accept (2) and (3) and so reject (1). The great question then is whether (1) can be denied without being forced to accept a Lockean analysis of particulars. For if the Lockean view is the only alternative to (1) then it may become more attractive to accept (1) and deny either (2) or (3). In ch. 11, however, I will argue that we can reject (1) without accepting the Lockean account of a particular. A particular's properties exhaust only its *nature*. It is an intelligible possibility that there should be two particulars with exactly the same nature. Yet this nature does not require a Lockean substratum.

Some philosophers will be dissatisfied with such an answer, and perhaps on good grounds. But it is very important to notice that the *Particularist* cannot object to it. For let us consider two of his particular *rednesses*, let them be of "exactly the same shade", and let them resemble each other in every other way. The Particularist must accept this as a possibility on pain of giving up (2). Now what makes the two particular *rednesses* two? Not substratum! The Particularist must either say that the two are barely numerically different, or else that they are made two by being at different places or place-times. But whichever of these answers he gives, he must in consistency allow that the Identity theorist can deny (1) without accepting substratum. For the Identity theorist can simply make the same answer.[1] So, whatever the usefulness and importance of recognizing that (1), (2) and (3) form an inconsistent triad, the subsequent attempted argument from (1) and (2) to the falsity of (3), is unavailable to the *Particularist*.

11 *Particularism and the Problem of Universals*

So the three arguments for Particularism fail, in each case instructively. The next step is to show that in arguing that the properties and relations of particulars are themselves particular the Particularist does not solve, but merely postpones, the Problem of Universals. Besides being grouped together in one way ("vertically", Williams) to form full-blooded or concrete things, Stoutian particulars are also grouped together in resemblance-classes ("horizontally", Williams), for instance, the class of all *rednesses* of this absolutely specific shade, the class of all *rednesses*, or the class of all

[1] See Brandt (1957), p. 528 n. 15.

colour-particulars. On what principle are these particulars thus grouped together into these classes?

It seems that the full range of answers to this problem is open to the Particularist. Predicate, Concept, Class, Mereological and Resemblance Nominalism, Transcendent Forms and Aristotelian (Immanent) Realism, all seem to be *prima facie* answers.

I do not know of any actual Particularist who has opted for a solution in terms of predicates or concepts. (Unless it be Aquinas. See the end of this chapter.) The difficulties brought up in chs. 2 and 3 for orthodox Predicate and Concept Nominalism appear to have exactly the same force when the particulars which fall under the common predicate or concept are thought of as Stoutian particulars. For instance, the particular *whitenesses* are not all treated as members of the one class simply because the predicate 'white' is applied to them all. Rather, the same predicate applies because they all have something in common. But what this common something is, a Predicate or Concept Nominalist cannot say.

The Class-membership analysis is represented by Stout himself. The universal, he said, is "a class or kind". The particular *redness* of this carpet is a member of a certain class of particulars: the class of all *rednesses*. In the Particularist context, the Class-membership analysis has one spectacular advantage. It eliminates the problem faced by an orthodox, non-Particularist, Class Nominalist: the difficulty about co-extensive properties. Let F and G be distinct but co-extensive properties. Let a be F and also be G. If a's being F and a's being G is analysed as a's being a member of the class of ordinary particulars which are F and which are also G, then we get the unwelcome result that F = G. But if Stoutian particulars are considered, then the class of *F-nesses* and the class of *G-nesses* are distinct classes, so that F ≠ G.

Nevertheless, all the other difficulties which we advanced against the orthodox Class-membership analysis still remain. It seems clear, for instance, that it is the nature of the members of the class that determines which class they belong to, rather than the class which they belong to determining their nature.

Did Stout want to maintain that *every* class of Stoutian particulars formed a kind? There is no clear answer in his writings. But the supposition seems an extremely implausible one. What unity has the class formed by the union of the class of particular smells with the class of particular triangular shapes? At any rate, Sotut says that "kinds", such as the class of particular *rednesses*, have a "distributive unity". The notion of a distributive unity, he goes on to say, is a fundamental one which cannot be further explained, although examples of other sorts of distributive unity can be given, such as the "vertical" unity of Stoutian particulars in a concrete thing. Stout specifically says that the distributive unity of a class or kind is not to be explained by the mutual resemblance of the members. The resemblance is determined by the distributive unity, not the unity by the resemblance.

But the notion of a distributive unity seems to be a restatement of Stout's problem rather than a solution of it. It is a way of saying that the members of certain classes of particulars are many, but at the same time one, while failing to explain what that oneness is. Certainly Stout seems in a very weak position to protest against an Identity theorist who takes it to be intelligible to say that members of the class of ordinary red particulars are one in respect of their *redness*.

Can the Particularist appeal to the *resemblance* of his classes of particulars? Among Particularists, the Resemblance solution seems to be favoured by Donald Williams. But it is given its most complete working out by Guido Küng, although he speaks of a relation of "equality" among his particulars rather than resemblance (Küng, 1964, 1967).

Like the Class-membership analysis, in the hands of a Particularist the Resemblance analysis yields one solid advantage over orthodox Resemblance Nominalism. (The advantage has been noted, in particular, by J. R. Jones, 1951.) We saw in criticizing Price's analysis that the fact that his paradigm objects are ordinary "thick" particulars led to trouble because of the indefinite multitude of properties such particulars possess. This opens up the permanent possibility that two objects may resemble the paradigms to the same degree, but that the resemblances may be in different respects. There seemed no way to eliminate this possibility. But in the Particularist version of the Resemblance analysis the paradigms will be Stoutian particulars, and these will not exhibit any such multitude of points of resemblance. So it will be relatively easy to provide a set of paradigms which exhibit the full range of the class in question yet which could not exhibit the full range of any other class.

But sufficient difficulties remain to overthrow the Particularist version of the Resemblance analysis completely. Here we may recall three. First, it seems clear that the relation of resemblance (or "equality") depends upon the nature of the object, not the nature of the object upon the relation. This difficulty is not considered by Küng, but is discussed by Jones (1951, pp. 560–2 especially) who argues that it is a decisive objection.

Second, the Resemblance analysis is involved in vicious regress. An account of the unity of a class of things which all "have the same property" appeals to the resemblance which each of these things has to suitable paradigms. Relations of resemblance have been substituted for the original property, simply recreating the old problem of universals in a new guise. An account of the unity of this class of Particularist relations of resemblance must again appeal to the resemblance of these relations, and so *ad infinitum*.

Küng (1964) admits that there is a regress, but claims that it is not vicious. The most he will concede is that it is ontologically a little extravagant. In our original discussion of Resemblance Nominalism, however, it was maintained that the regress was vicious. The situation seems unchanged when it is Particularism which is being considered. Each level of the regress leaves us with a new form of the very problem it was supposed to have solved at the level immediately below.

Third, it is perfectly intelligible that a particular may be the only one of its kind, and so have nothing to resemble or be "equal" to. Küng considers this difficulty (1967, p. 173 n. 28). In reply he appeals to "the thomistic doctrine of real possibility". I take it that he is trying to meet the difficulty by appealing to *possible* particulars to which the actual particular has the relation of "equality". As already urged on other occasions, the remedy is a truly desperate one.

So much for Nominalist solutions to the One over Many problem as it presents itself to a Particularist. Particularism could also be combined with Realism. However, I know of no Particularist who has appealed to transcendent Forms. All the difficulties in this case which exist for a non-Particularist theory of properties appear to obtain in the Particularist case also.

So finally we come to the attempt to combine Particularism with Immanent Realism. This is the view which seems to be taken by Cook Wilson (1926), Kemp Smith (1927) and Jones (1951). They hold that particular properties, such as particular rednesses, have intrinsic, objective, properties in the traditional or universalistic sense of "property". Each particular *redness* has the non-particular property of redness (and so the concrete particular in question may also be said to have the non-particular property).

Such a view is certainly more satisfactory than a *Nominalist* Particularism. But it is hard to see what advantages this Realist view has over a *simple* Identity analysis. If Immanent Realism is satisfactory on the second time round, then what intellectual motive is there for resisting it first time round? One must drop the argument that if two different things each have the same property, then a property will be at two different places at the same time and so will be divided from itself. We have seen that Particularism gives no special advantage in accounting for reference to such things as "the redness of this carpet". Every consideration of economy seems to plead for the elimination of the Particularist properties. They are a useless intermediary between ordinary particulars and their universal properties.

III *The incoherence of Particularism*

Can we go further than this? Is the Particularist assumption actually incoherent? There is reason to think it is. I will advance two arguments against Particularism. The first is not decisive, but I think that the second is.

First, it seems clear that the very same particular cannot instantiate a property more than once. To say that *a* is F *and* that *a* is F is simply to say that *a* is F. Given the Identity view of properties, this is immediately explicable. For a Particularist, however, an ordinary concrete particular is a collection of Stoutian particulars. Why should not this collection contain two Stoutian particulars which resemble exactly? But this will be equivalent to saying that the concrete particular has the same property twice over. The Particularist can only meet this difficulty by introducing an *ad hoc* principle forbidding exactly resembling Stoutian particulars to be parts of the same concrete particular.

The second argument depends upon the premiss, already argued for, that Particularism about properties and relations must be supplemented by an Immanent Realism. Only so can we explain how Stoutian particulars can be classed and sorted. Let us suppose, then, that a particular *yellowness*, say *the yellowness of this lemon*, has the universal property, *being a certain shade of yellow*. The *redness of this tomato*, however, does not have this universal property. The question is: is there any reason present in the nature of the first Stoutian particular, but lacking in the nature of the second Stoutian particular, why the first particular has this universal property? If there is no reason, then it seems that the Stoutian particulars, in abstraction from their universal properties, are mere bare particulars. This would make the different Stoutian properties of a thing, in abstraction from their universal properties, indistinguishable from each other, which seems absurd. But if the nature of the first Stoutian particular is not bare and so "fits" *being a certain shade of yellow*, while the nature of the second particular does not, must not the nature of the two particulars already be something universal? Could not the nature of *the yellowness of this lemon* be duplicated in another lemon? But then *the yellowness of this lemon* is not, after all, a particular but a universal and no further universal is required.[1]

At this point I think that the Particularist view of properties and relations must be finally and completely abandoned.

Before leaving this topic, we may take brief notice of the Scholastic view that essences (very roughly: properties) are neither universal nor particular. Sometimes this view is glossed by saying that the essence is universal in the mind (that is, as a concept) but particular in the thing. This looks like the adoption of Particularism together with Concept Nominalism. *Perhaps* this is the position of Aquinas.[2]

At other times, however, it is said that the essence in the thing is more than a particular but less than a universal. This seems to be the view of Scotus. For Scotus, each man, for instance, has a nature, and this nature is a "common nature". That suggests that essences are universals. Nevertheless, Scotus holds, by comparison with the identity of particulars the unity (identity) involved is a "lesser unity". I find this view difficult to understand. It appears to imply the doctrine that identity of particulars, on the one hand, and identity of properties and relations, on the other, involve different senses of the word "identity". I will comment upon the latter view in ch. 11 § 11.

---

[1] See Blanshard's brilliant critique of Kemp Smith's view (1939, p. 595, n. 1).
[2] See, for instance, Francis P. Clarke's account (1962) of Aquinas' view on universals. Clarke concludes that "universality is only a logical function of predication, that is, of discursive thought".

PART THREE
PARTICULARS

9

Are particulars reducible to universals?

We have now investigated and rejected those analyses of what it is for a particular to have a certain property which construe this as a *relation* between the thing and something else distinct from it. *a*'s being F is not a matter of *a* falling under the predicate 'F'; it is not a matter of *a* falling under the concept *F*; it is not a matter of *a* being a member of the class of the Fs; it is not a matter of *a* being a part of the aggregate of the Fs; it is not a matter of *a* having a suitable resemblance to a set of paradigm particulars; it is not a matter of *a* "participating" in the Form of F. (By implication, we have also rejected similar analyses of what it is for *a* to have a relation, R, to other particulars.) The conclusion is that a particular's properties are intrinsic to the thing itself. Furthermore, we have seen these properties cannot be conceived of as (first-order) particulars. They are universals.

But if we have to admit universals, motives of intellectual economy will naturally lead us to see how much work they are able to do. So we should now investigate the view, already christened "Universalism" in ch. 2 § 1, that an account can be given of particulars solely in terms of universals. In particular, we must investigate the view that particulars are nothing but "bundles" of properties.

The view is to be found in the later Russell (1940, ch. 6, 1948, Part II, ch. 3 and Part IV, ch. 8, 1959, ch. 9; see also Loux, forthcoming), in Blanshard (1939, ch. 17, 1962, ch. 9) and Hochberg (1965, 1966, 1969). Russell (1948) attributes the view to Leibniz, but, while the influence of Leibniz on Russell is clear, it is less clear that Leibniz held this theory of the nature of particulars. Of course, the theory must be sharply distinguished from the Particularist view that a particular is a bundle of properties which are themselves (first-order) particulars, a view rejected by implication in the previous chapter when this view of properties was rejected.

Drawing the distinction between the two theories is not made any easier by Russell himself, who speaks of his properties (more usually "qualities") as particulars. Russell, however, is not putting forward the Particularist view. (Still less does he hold the Mereological view that redness, say, is the aggregate or collection of all the red things.) Russell calls his qualities "particulars" because (a) they are the ultimate subjects of predication and the ultimate terms of relations – they play the role of "substance" in his theory; (b) they themselves, according to Russell, fall under universals—for instance, he holds that the shades of colour fall under the universal *colour*. I do not think that either of those considerations is sufficient for saying that his qualities are particulars. Certainly, as Russell freely concedes, they behave very like traditional universals. Hence I take the liberty of treating Russell's theory as one which seeks to construct (ordinary) particulars from universals. Russell's view, as he expounds it, also gets mixed up with a good deal of epistemological material about sense-fields which is not important for our purposes.

His fundamental device is to introduce an unanalysable, symmetrical, non-transitive relation which holds between some, but not all, pairs of properties. Russell calls the relation "compresence". A "complex of compresence" is then a class of properties each member of which is compresent with each other member. A *complete* complex of compresence is one where there exists no further property which is compresent with each member of the class. Particulars are then identified with complete complexes of compresence.

A model for a complex of compresence is a mutual admiration society, where it is a condition of membership that each member admires each other member. The society may be enlarged to the point where no further member can be added and the society remain a mutual admiration society. It then serves as a model for a *complete* complex of compresence. Notice that there might be a particular mutual admiration society to which A could be added, and nobody further, and to which B could be added, and nobody further. A and B could not both be added to the society because A and B do not stand in the relation of mutual admiration. But two societies could be formed, with overlapping membership, the original society, plus A without B, and the original society plus B without A. Complete complexes of compresence might overlap in the same way.

It may be noticed that the relation of *compresence* yields conjunctions of properties in the same particular(s). It will be argued further in ch. 15 § 1, that a conjunction of properties, provided it is actually instantiated, is itself a property. If this is correct, then complexes of compresence, including complete complexes of compresence, are themselves properties. So a particular is simultaneously a (conjunctive) property. I think that Russell himself accepted this consequence.

1 *The Identity of Indiscernibles*

Four arguments will be advanced against the view that a particular is nothing but a bundle of properties which are universals. The first is traditional: that this account of particulars requires the truth of the Principle of the Identity of Indiscernibles, but that there are good reasons to reject this Principle. Second, it will be argued that the theory unwarrantably excludes particulars whose properties form a sub-class of the properties which make up another particular. Third, it will be argued that there can be complete complexes of compresence, as defined by Russell, in the absence of the corresponding particular. Fourth, it will be argued that a Bundle view runs into difficulties with the *parts* of particulars. Our present business is with the first objection.

I begin by setting out a traditional argument.

If it is true that a particular is a bundle of properties, and if properties are universals, then these truths are necessarily true. If so, then, necessarily, if particulars *a* and *b* have exactly the same properties, then *a* and *b* are the very same particular.[1] That is to say, the Identity of Indiscernibles is necessarily true. As we will see in a moment, the Identity of Indiscernibles can be given more than one interpretation. But on no interpretation does it appear to be a necessary truth. It cannot be denied that it is necessarily true that properties are universals (see ch. 8). So it cannot be a necessary truth that a particular is a bundle of universals. But if this is not a necessary truth, it is not a truth at all.

[1] Extraordinarily, this appears to be denied by Hochberg (1969) p. 191.

As I have said, the line of argument given above is a traditional one, although in the past no very careful attention has been paid to the modal character of the argument. It does suffer from the disadvantage that Russell, at least, shows signs of thinking that the identification of particulars with bundles of properties is a *contingent* truth. He regards himself as committed to the Identity of Indiscernibles, but not always, apparently, to its necessity. So it will be important in what follows not simply to argue against the necessity of the Identity of Indiscernibles, but also against the view that it is true at all.

The Identity of Indiscernibles (or Dissimilarity of the Diverse as McTaggart helpfully calls it: 1921, § xcix) can be given two interpretations. We first divide properties into non-relational and relational properties. (We must, of course, distinguish relational properties from relations.) According to the *Strong* form of the Identity of Indiscernibles, different particulars must differ in at least some non-relational properties. According to the *Weak* form of the Principle, different particulars must differ in at least some properties, but these need only be relational properties.

My line of argument will be this. (1) It is easy to see that the Strong form of the Principle is not a necessary truth. So if the Bundle theory requires the necessity of the Strong Principle, then it is easily refuted. (2) There are scientific grounds for thinking that the Strong Principle is not true at all. (3) The Bundle theory requires the Strong Principle. An attempt to work with the Weak Principle involves the Bundle theory in circularity. (4) There are cases which seem to show that not even the Weak Principle is a necessary truth.

(1) *The Strong form of the Principle is not a necessary truth.* If we consider two ordinary particulars, two ball-bearings say, whose non-relational properties appear to be exactly the same, then we believe that a sufficiently detailed examination will reveal internal differences. But it is surely conceivable, surely logically possible, that there are no such differences.

In defence of the necessity of the (Strong) Principle it may be objected that two objects, *a* and *b*, will necessarily differ in at least one non-relational property. *a* has the property, *being identical with a*, but lacks the property, *being identical with b*. With *b* the situation is reversed.

However, this defence hardly inspires confidence. First, *being identical with a* and *being identical with b* are not properties, if properties are universals. For they lack a necessary mark of universals, the logical possibility that the class of particulars which have this property be an infinite class. Universals are potential ones *over many*. *Being identical with itself* would have this mark of a universal (although I think that there are other grounds for denying that there is such a property), but *a* and *b* are *each* identical with themselves and so are not discernible in this respect. Second, the *Bundle* theory of particulars could not regard *being identical with a* as a property of *a*. For its object is to give an account of *a* in terms of its properties. But this "property" involves the very thing which the theory seeks to analyse: the particular *a* itself.

Again, it may be objected, in defence of the necessity of the Strong Principle, that different particulars necessarily differ in spatio-temporal position. I will be arguing in ch. 11 § v that it is possible that there are particulars which occupy exactly the same spatio-temporal position. It is logically possible, also, that there are particulars which are not spatio-temporal at all, and so do not differ in position. For the present, however, I waive both these replies to the present objection. Instead I ask whether difference in spatio-temporal position can be a difference in *property*?

If spatio-temporal position is definable in relational terms, perhaps it involves differences in relational properties. But this is not to our purpose here. The Strong Principle, whose alleged necessity we are currently examining, concerns non-relational properties. Nor can we appeal to the non-relational properties of the objects which occupy different positions. For we have already noted that it is logically possible that such objects might not differ in non-relational properties. But if we abstract from both the relational and the non-relational properties of the things which have spatio-temporal position, surely whatever is left – "the spatio-temporal positions themselves" – do not differ in *nature*, i.e. in their repeatable properties, in any way? It is clear, at least, that they *need* not differ in nature. So it seems that position is no beter than self-identity at providing a necessary point of internal difference for different particulars.

We may conclude, then, that the Strong form of the Identity of Indiscernibles is not a necessary truth.

(2) *The Strong form of the Principle may not be true at all.* We believe that, at the macroscopic level, any two objects will, as a

matter of fact, exhibit some internal differences. But it is noteworthy that our confidence in differences at the macroscopic level does not extend to the microscopic constituents out of which (or so Scientific Realists about the entities of physics believe) macroscopic objects are made up. Might there not be two electrons with the very same non-relational properties? Leibniz used the Principle to attack the hypothesis of indiscernible atoms, but this seems to be intolerable *a priorism*.

Writing in the *Scientific American*, Weinberg (1974) had this to say:

> as far as we know, any two [elementary] particles of the same species are, except for their position and state of motion, absolutely identical, whether they occupy the same atom or lie at opposite ends of the universe. (p. 50)

We have already discussed, and rejected, the claim of position to provide internal differentiation. It would seem to be physically possible for two particles of the same species to be in exactly the same state of motion. So there appear to be scientific reasons for thinking that the strong form of the Principle is actually false.

(3) *The Weak form of the Principle involves the Bundle theory in circularity*. Can the Bundle theorist appeal to the Weak form of the Principle of the Identity of Indiscernibles? Conceding that it is logically (and even empirically) possible that two particulars should have all their non-relational properties in common, could he go on to maintain that, if relational properties are included, particulars logically must exhibit differences in property?[1]

What will count as a relational property from the point of view of the Bundle theory? It may be true of *a* that it is to the left of *b*. But *being to the left of b* will not be a suitable relational property. For *b* is a particular, and the project is to give an account of particulars purely in terms of properties. It seems that the required properties must be such things as *being to the left of a lamp post* or *above something orange*.

But even if we only consider relational properties of this latter sort, the Bundle theory still seems involved in circularity. The relational properties of a particular will be a matter of its having relations to other particulars of a certain sort. But the notion of a

[1] There is a long, deep and difficult discussion of this issue in Hochberg (1969, Part II).

particular is the notion to be analysed. So the Bundle theorist must analyse the situation where a particular has a relational property by saying that one bundle of properties has a certain relation to another bundle of properties.

Every relational property that a particular has, then, will be a matter of a bundle of properties standing in a certain relation to other bundles of properties. The bundles of properties themselves will therefore have to be bundles of *non-relational* properties. Only so can there be bundles to have relations to other bundles. Each of these bundles is a different particular, so no two bundles can contain exactly the same non-relational properties. That is to say, the Bundle theory is forced to appeal to the *Strong* version of the Identity of Indiscernibles. Relational properties cannot be used to differentiate particulars. But we have seen that the *Strong* form of the Principle is not a necessary truth, and may not even be true.

(4) *The Weak form of the Principle is not a necessary truth.* If the previous argument is sound, discussion of the Weak form of the Principle is irrelevant. But perhaps it is not sound. It may therefore be worth showing that even the Weak Principle is not a necessary truth. There seem to be logically possible cases where the Principle fails to hold.

The argument is not quite conclusive, because the cases are somewhat *recherché*. This fact makes it just possible to uphold the principle against the cases and take the latter to be impossible. But, on considering the cases, it seems clear that, if we have to choose between calling the cases incoherent or the Principle false, then, other considerations being equal, it is the Principle which should be rejected. Three cases will be mentioned.

(1) Max Black (1952, p. 161) writes:

suppose ... that we have ... a *centre* of symmetry. I mean that everything that happened at any place would be duplicated at a place an equal distance on the opposite side of the centre of symmetry. In short, the universe would be what mathematicians call "radially symmetrical". And to avoid complications we could suppose that the centre of symmetry itself was physically inaccessible, so that it would be impossible for any material body to pass through it.

(2) A. J. Ayer (1954, p. 34) gives a second case. It is that of a universe, which could be ours, which has repeated and will repeat

itself in exactly the same fashion from and to infinity. The boundary-conditions in a deterministic universe might bring it about that the universe went through such eternal repetition.

Russell appears to have considered cases of the sort given by Black and Ayer. He responded by denying that there are:

> any spatial or temporal relations which always and necessarily imply diversity.[1]

What I take to be his meaning may be best brought out by considering Ayer's case. I think that Russell would interpret Ayer's allegedly cyclic universe as a case where time "came round upon itself". It is not the case that event *a* is eventually followed by its twin event *a'*, but rather that *a* is followed by *a* itself.

Russell's way of putting the point involves the difficult notion of reflexive relation, which we will not be discussing (and rejecting) until ch. 19 § vi. But the point can be put less controversially. Given that time is a linear order, it may still be the case that for two distinct events, *a* and *b*, which are not simultaneous, each of them is before (and after) the other.

I think Russell is right to point to this possibility. He is right also to point out, as he does (1959, pp. 164–5), that it is a desirable advance towards empiricism to see that time does not logically have to be open-ended. But does he not himself sin against empiricism when he contends, as he appears to, that Ayer's case *must* be interpreted as a case of circular time? It seems to me that there are two possible cases: Russell's case and Ayer's case. Time might be circular. Alternatively, the same sort of events might recur forever, without numerical identity. After all, it is only required that Ayer's case be possible. That is sufficient to disprove the necessity of the Weak Principle.

(3) Finally C. D. Broad (1933, pp. 176–7) has argued that, *pace* Kant, it is not a necessary truth that there is only one spatio-temporal system. Might there not be two, or more, and might they not be exactly alike? The interest of this case is that it excludes any such reply like that urged by Russell against the two other cases.

Ayer admits the force of the cases but is still inclined to uphold

---

[1] See *Logic and Knowledge*, ed. R. C. Marsh (1956), p. 124 (paragraph added to Russell, 1911).

the Principle against the cases. He argues that the only alternative to saying that a particular is nothing but a bundle of properties is the Lockean view that particulars contain an unknowable substratum which is the bearer of these properties. He prefers the deep blue sea of the Identity of Indiscernibles to the Lockean devil. However, it will be argued in the next chapter that the situation is not as Ayer represents it to be. We can reject both the Identity of Indiscernibles and the doctrine of substratum. If so, we can use the cases against the view that the Weak Principle is a necessary truth.

It must be admitted finally, however, that the Weak form of the Principle appears to be in fact true. Perhaps it can be shown, contrary to my argument a few pages back, that the *Strong* form of the Principle is not required for the Bundle theory. If, further, the Bundle theory could be maintained as a mere matter of fact, and not as a necessity, then the cases of Black, Ayer and Broad might be ignored. After all, they carry little conviction except as mere possibilities.

The discussion has been long and complex. But, with the reservation made in the previous paragraph, it seems that the traditional line of criticism of the Bundle theory can be made good.

II *Another argument against the Bundle theory*

If something is a particular if and only if it is a complete complex of compresent properties, then a complex of compresent properties which is not complete is not a particular. But now consider any particular, for instance, a certain lump of metal. Might there not be another particular having no properties except ones which the original particular possessed, but which lacked some of the properties possessed by the first particular – its visual properties, say? The supposition seems easy and natural. Yet the Bundle theory, as formulated by Russell, must deny that the second particular could exist. For its properties are a sub-class of the properties of the lump of metal, and so the second particular would not be a *complete* complex of compresent properties.

Russell could avoid this result by introducing negative properties. If an object lacks the property, P, then it possesses the property, *not being P*. If this is granted, the two classes of properties associated with the two particulars in the previous example will merely overlap, which the theory can accept. In ch. 14 § 11, however, I hope to show that there are many good reasons for rejecting negative properties.

It is not possible to meet the difficulty by dropping the requirement that a particular be a *complete* complex of compresence. If this requirement is waived, then, for each complex of compresence contained within a complete complex of compresence, there must exist a distinct particular. But it is obviously possible that such particulars need not exist. The difficulty is the mirror-image of the difficulty proposed for Russell's original definition of a particular.

It may, however, be replied that a complete complex of compresence, such as the lump of metal, contains each of the required complexes of compresence *within itself* – as a sort of part of the lump of metal. This would provide for the existence of each complex of compresence as a particular without being committed to anything except the lump of metal. This reply, however, would only reinstate the original difficulty. For then, by the Identity of Indiscernibles, there can be no *other* particulars, outside the lump of metal, which have all and only the properties which make up these (mere) complexes of compresence. Yet why should there not be such particulars?

I conclude that, whether particulars are defined as complete complexes of compresence, or merely as complexes of compresence, the theory either enjoins or forbids the existence of particulars of certain sorts in a quite arbitrary manner.

III *Two further objections*

In a paper (1975) I put forward an argument against the Bundle theory which I now think fails. But Michael Tooley has produced a not-too-dissimilar argument which seems to succeed. Let there be a particular, a, which, among its properties, has P, Q and lacks R. b has Q, R and lacks P. c has P, R and lacks Q. Let it also be nomically impossible that any particular have all the properties P, Q and R. It seems clear that all these four conditions might be jointly satisfied.

Yet Russell cannot allow that they are jointly satisfied. P is compresent with Q, Q with R, and P with R. They form a "mutual admiration society", a complex of compresence. So they must either constitute a complete complex of compresence or a mere complex of compresence. But the fourth condition entails that there is no such complex.

Tooley suggests that this difficulty be met by changing Russell's definition of a particular. Let *Compresent* (P, Q) entail merely that there exists an x such that x is P and is Q; C(Q, R) entail merely that there exists a y such that y is Q and is R; C (P,R) entail merely that there exists a z such that z is P and is R. The conjunction of these premisses does not entail that x, y and z are identical, and so does not entail that there is a particular which is P, Q and R. (P, Q), (Q, R) and (P, R) are then conceived of as conjunctive properties, and it is allowed that these conjunctive properties may, or may not, have the compresence relation, C, to further properties. Suppose, in our case, C((P, Q)R), C((Q, R)P) and finally C((P, R)Q). Then there will be a w such that w is P, is Q and is R. Following out an analogy with a power-set, we may speak of a "power" admiration society. In such a society, not merely does each member of the society admire each of the others, but each sub-group in the society, including unit sub-groups, admires each other sub-group. It is this sort of relation that Tooley demands hold between the different properties of a *single* particular.

But this new construction is not without its difficulties either. If there is a particular having properties P, Q and R then, according to Tooley, three relations hold: C((P, Q)R); C((P, R)Q); C((Q, R)P). To deny that any of the three relations hold seems arbitrary. (The situation where all three relations hold is the one modelled by the "power" admiration society.) Nevertheless, relations of compresence between different relata are presumably independent of each other. So one or more of these three relational situations might obtain without the others. But what interpretation can be placed upon the statement that, say, (P, R) is compresent with Q, but not (P, Q) with R or (Q, R) with P? We still get an object having P, Q and R. So what is the difference between this situation and the one where all three relational situations obtain?

Another suggestion for modifying Russell's view is this. We distinguish between classes and aggregates of particulars. An aggregate of particulars may have a property that no member of the corresponding class has. The notion of an aggregate of properties is a much more difficult one, but perhaps it can be admitted. Particulars are now considered to be aggregates of properties (monadic universals). What marks off particulars from other aggregates of properties, such as, say, the aggregate of all the colours? Not certain relations between the parts of the aggregate (in effect, the Russell and Tooley suggestions). Instead, it may be suggested, those and only those aggregates which are particulars have a common property, call it A. Possession of A constitutes their particularity.

This suggestion is jejune and unintuitive. But it does seem to escape the present difficulty. It may be noted, however, that the suggestion would still have to face the difficulties brought up in § I about the Identity of Indiscernibles. Again, the difficulty raised in § II could be reformulated against this new version of the Bundle theory.

A fourth objection to the Bundle theory I owe to Geoffrey Harris. It is clear that many properties of particulars involve essential reference to proper parts of these particulars. If a thing is to be a chess-board, for instance, it must have spatial parts of a certain nature related in a certain way. These parts, however, are particulars. It appears, then, that many of the properties which figure in the bundle involve the notion of further particulars. Yet the notion of a particular is the one to be analysed.

Presumably the Bundle theorist will reply that these further particulars are themselves bundles of properties. But these new bundles may themselves include properties which involve reference to still further parts, which are again particulars. Now it is at least logically possible that this process should go on *ad infinitum*. A particular may lack any ultimate parts. But for such particulars, it is suggested, it is impossible to carry out the resolution of particulars into bundles of properties.

Like all arguments depending upon infinite regress, this argument is difficult to evaluate. But it is certainly worth consideration.

I conclude that, in this chapter, a strong case has been made out for denying that particulars are nothing but bundles of properties conceived of as universals. We must reject Universalism as well as Nominalism. Notice, yet again, that none of the arguments given has any force against the conception of a thing as a bundle of properties conceived as particulars. I rely on the arguments of the previous chapter to refute such a notion of properties (and relations).

It remains true that if we compare Nominalism, the attempt to reduce universals to particulars, with Universalism, the attempt to reduce particulars to universals, the former attempt, however misguided, seems to have an intellectual naturalness which is lacking in the latter. In ch. 11 § III, I call attention to a phenomenon which I call "the victory of particularity". Though it does not justify Nominalism, I think it goes far to explain this asymmetry.

10

The Lockean account of particulars

It is not possible to give an account of properties and relations purely in terms of particulars. That is the error of Nominalism. It is not possible to give an account of particulars purely in terms of (universal) properties. That is the error of Universalism. We must admit *both* particulars and universals.

This admission is the beginning of wisdom, but it is only the beginning. For the question which then arises is the way in which particulars and universals stand to each other. We must first reject Transcendent Realism, the doctrine that universals stand outside particulars in a realm apart. This has already been criticized in ch. 7. But if Transcendent Realism is rejected, then some version of Immanent Realism must be accepted.

We do normally think of a particular as something "containing" its properties (or at least its non-relational properties). But since a particular is not exhausted by its properties, it also has a particularity which, together with its properties, goes to make up the whole particular. The question then is: how are we to conceive of this union of particularity and universality in a particular?

A natural first thought is that particularity and universality are related constituents of particulars. We may call it the *Relational* form of Immanent Realism. The object of this chapter is to criticize this form of Immanent Realism.

This line of thought is the deepest source of the doctrine that particulars involve an unknowable substratum which stands in the relation of support to its properties, or is that in which the properties inhere (support and inherence being the converses of each other). Substratum is simply the particularity of particulars conceived of as a constituent of a particular, a constituent which must be related to the properties of the particular.

Ayer (1954, p. 35) gives as his reason for clinging to the doctrine of the Identity of Indiscernibles his suspicion of "the category of substance". By "substance" he appears to understand "substratum". It is true that the doctrine of a substratum has other sources. Locke, for instance, was deeply impressed by our ignorance of the real nature of physical objects (an ignorance which is now a little less than it was in the seventeenth century). So for him substratum tends to merge with that unknown nature. But to speak of the nature of a thing, whether the nature be known or unknown, is to speak of the properties of that thing. The metaphysical substratum, on the other hand, supports, but must be distinguished from, any properties of the thing. Our concern is with the metaphysical substratum.

I speak of a "Lockean" analysis for convenience. But, of course, Locke is a Nominalist. Hence, when he speaks of the substratum supporting properties, he cannot in consistency think of these properties as universals. I have no evidence that he ever considered the matter, but his properties ought to be particularized or Stoutian properties. Our concern, on the contrary, is with properties as universals.

1 *Unsound criticisms of the Lockean account*

Before embarking upon criticisms, I shall briefly mention two objections to the doctrine which do not seem to be sound. M. J. Loux (1974, p. 773) argues against the postulation of a substratum by saying:

> the conception of an object which in itself lacks all characteristics is incoherent; for we cannot say what we mean by such an object unless we do, in fact, attribute a characteristic to it – the characteristic of being in itself without all characteristics.

It is undoubtedly true that, if there are Lockean substrata, the predicate 'without all characteristics' applies to them. But why does it follow that this predicate must apply in virtue of a *characteristic* (property) of the substratum? This would only follow if every predicate which applies to an object must apply in virtue of characteristics of the object. This further doctrine itself follows from the identification of characteristics with the meanings of predicates, the identification made by the Argument from Meaning.

It will be argued in Part Four that the Argument from Meaning is unsound, and that, once it is seen to be unsound, there is no need to assume that in each case in which a predicate applies it applies in virtue of characteristics. Once this assumption is given up, we are free to consider in individual cases, and on the merit of the case, whether the predicate does apply in virtue of characteristics. Now a predicate like 'without all characteristics' inspires no confidence at all. It is natural to say that the absence of characteristics is not a characteristic. (I shall in fact be arguing in detail in Part Four that there are no negative properties at all.) I therefore reject Loux's argument.

It may also be argued that the substratum must, by hypothesis, have one property, the relational property, *supporting properties and relations*. But if it has this property, it is not propertyless.

This argument cannot be accepted either. I shall discuss relational properties in ch. 19 § 11. It will be argued there that, although relational properties are real, they are nothing over and above the relations which objects have to other objects having certain (non-relational) properties. So to say that the substratum has the relational property, *supporting properties*, is to say nothing more than this: that it and its properties are related by the relation of *support*. This is the original hypothesis, and therefore no contradiction has been deduced from it.

11 *What is the relation between substratum and properties?*

In discussing the theory of Forms we saw that it is not possible to characterize the relation which is supposed to hold between particular and Form. If the words "participation" and "imitation" are taken literally, then it is clear that they do not capture the nature of the relation. But if the words are taken analogically, then it is impossible to specify the point of resemblance to literal participation and imitation. In Aristotle's phrase, they are "empty metaphors". Furthermore, once we reject the notion that the Form of F has the property, *being F* (and if we do not reject this notion then a disastrous regress ensues), then we cannot say what the Form is like either. So it seems that the theory of Forms explains *a*'s being F by reference to *a*'s having a relation of which we are unable to give any concrete account to an object of which we are unable to give any concrete account. We are explaining the known by the unknown.

The same difficulty may be developed in connection with the doctrine of substratum. The *locus classicus* is in Berkeley's writings. He argues that "support" and "inherence" are just as much empty metaphors in the case of substratum as we have seen "participation" and "imitation" to be in the case of Forms (*Principles*, 16–17 (especially), 68–81, and the *First Dialogue*).

Berkeley points out that we cannot take the words "support" and "inherence" literally. The substratum is not underneath the properties as pillars are underneath a roof, nor do they inhere in the substratum as burrs inhere in wool. But if the words are not to be taken literally, how are they to be taken? All we can say about the relation is that it is the relation which holds between the substratum and the properties. Nor can we say anything of interest about the substratum. Locke described it as "something I know not what", but that is in fact too flattering a description! It suggests that the substratum has a what, has a nature, although we cannot penetrate to that nature. But in fact it can have no nature. It is pure particularity, pure lack of nature standing in an indescribable relation to the properties. It is not clear that we have got an intelligible hypothesis here.

In the parallel situation with the theory of Forms, it is natural, once the difficulty is perceived, to cut away the mysterious objects to which particulars have an inexplicable relation, and content ourselves with the particulars themselves. For what explanatory value can these Forms have? Similarly, it is natural to cut away the mysterious substratum to which properties have an inexplicable relation, and content ourselves with the properties themselves. This, however, leads to the difficulties of the Bundle theory discussed in the last chapter.

However, as already pointed out in ch. 7 § 11, the difficulty proposed for the theory of Forms, although persuasive, is not completely compelling. It is open to a defender of the theory to say (with Cook Wilson) that the relation is *sui generis*, that the Form is also something *sui generis*, but that anybody who grasps that a thing has a certain property is acquainted, however unselfconsciously, with Forms and the relation which they bear to particulars.

In the same way, it can be replied to Berkeley that the relation of *support* is *sui generis*, that the substratum is something *sui generis*, but that anybody who grasps that a thing has a property is

acquainted, however unselfconsciously, with substrata and the
relation which they bear to properties.

III *Another infinite regress*

It will now be argued, however, that the view that a particular is
composed of a substratum related in a certain fashion to properties
(conceived of as universals) is involved in vicious regress.

If a substratum of a particular requires to be bound by a relation
("support") to a *property* of that particular, then, equally, if a substratum enters into a *relation* with something, the substratum will
require a relation to bind it to that relation. Suppose, for instance,
that two ordinary particulars are related. Will not the two substrata
of the two particulars require relations to bind each of them to the
relation? To deny this, but to assert that the substratum and the
property of a particular must be related, would be to make a quite
arbitrary distinction between monadic universals (properties) and
polyadic universals (relations).

But now consider the relation R ("support") which holds between
the substratum and the properties of the same particular. Even if the
properties require no further relation to relate them to R, the
substratum will require such a relation (which may or may not be
of just the same sort as that holding between substratum and
properties). A regress clearly ensues. The regress is a sign that
the original postulation of R holding between substratum and
properties simply reproduces the problem it was supposed to solve.
That is to say, the regress is vicious. And if no second relation
is required to bind the substratum and R together, why was R
required to bring together substrata and properties in the first
place?

The regress just developed against the Relational version of
Immanent Realism is one of the regresses deployed by Bradley
(1897, ch. 3). It is similar to the "Relation" regress used in this book
against each of the various forms of Nominalism together with the
doctrine of transcendent universals. Fairly clearly, Bradley's argument and the Relation regresses either stand together (as I have
argued) or else fall together. Even if they fall and none of them is
logically vicious, in each case an ontological regress to infinity is
involved. In the case of the present argument, a substratum has R to
its properties, R′ (which may or may not be type-identical with R)

to R, R″ to R′ and so *ad infinitum.* The substratum theory is thus, at best, viciously uneconomical.

It seems that what is required is some more intimate union between the particularity and universality of particulars than mere relation. We require a *non-relational* form of Immanent Realism.

I I

Particulars and universals

We have now reached a turning-point. Up to this moment our primary concern has been to criticize opposed standpoints: the doctrine that everything is a particular, that there are transcendent universals, that properties and relations are particulars, that particulars are constructions out of universal properties, that particulars contain two constituents – their particularity and their universality —which have to be related. From this moment on, although criticism of alternatives will remain important, the primary concern will be to advance a positive account of particulars and universals.

I *The properties of a particular are not related to that particular*

Of the various accounts of the nature of particulars which we have considered, the form of Immanent Realism examined in the last chapter comes closest to being satisfactory. But it errs in making the particularity of particulars into a separate constituent of the particular – the substratum – which must then be related to another constituent – the universals instantiated by the particular. What is required instead is a *non-relational* Immanent Realism.

Consider the old dilemma. Given different things with the same property, then the property must be either partially or wholly present in the things. If partially, then the unity of the property is destroyed. But if wholly in each, how can it be in either? This argument has nourished both Nominalism, and also Particularism about properties.

If we are forced to take one horn of this dilemma, then I think it is clear that we should take the second. If two things have the very same property, then that property is, in some sense, "in" each of them. But this does not mean that the properties of a thing are separate constituents of the thing.

Instead we must just stick with this proposition: different particulars may have the same property. (And different pairs, triples, etc. of particulars may have the same relation.) Different particulars may be (wholly or partially) identical in nature. Such identity in nature is literally inexplicable, in the sense that it cannot be further explained. But that does not make it incoherent. Identity in nature entails that the universe is unified in a way that the Nominalist finds unintuitive. But I take that to be simply the fault of the Nominalist's intuitions.

We simply have to accept that different particulars may have the same property or be related by the same relation. But, as we shall see, this does not open the door to Realist excess. It is compatible with the recognition that not every predicate which applies to many particulars applies in virtue of a universal, and that painful and extensive enquiry is necessary to determine what the properties and relations of a particular are. Diogenes told Plato that he could see the horse but not *horseness*. A scientific Realism might come to agree with Diogenes about the particular case, even while insisting that different particulars *can* have identical natures.

However, the substitution of *a posteriori* for *a priori* Realism is a new theme. Leaving it aside for the present, I note that this version of Immanent Realism which distinguishes the particularity from the properties of a particular, while denying that the two aspects are related, constitutes the "great tradition" of Realistic thought about universals. Aristotle can be claimed as its founder, with his doctrine that the least thing capable of independent existence is a "this-such". A central figure is Duns Scotus, allowing no more than a "formal distinction", which is, however, a real distinction, between the this-ness (*haecceity*) of a particular and its "forms". In this century, the tradition is represented, in different ways, by such thinkers as W. E. Johnson (1921, Part I, ch. 1 § v and ch. 13 §§ iv and v), John Anderson (1962, ch. 11), Gustav Bergmann (1964, 1967) and P. F. Strawson (1959, ch. 5 § viii). A recent restatement of the view is to be found in Donagan (1963). It appears, furthermore, that the Nyāya and Vaiśeṣika schools of Indian philosophers held a similar view (see Chakrabarti, 1975). Reading this article, late in the composition of my book, provided a salutary shock to Western provinciality.

Johnson, Bergmann and Strawson all speak of a "tie" between particulars and universals (though Strawson speaks of a "non-relational" tie). This seems to me to be unfortunate terminology. It suggests that selfsame relational Immanent Realism which these thinkers are trying to get away from. Far more satisfactory is Scotus' "formal distinction" (see Boler, 1963, ch. 2 and Wolter, 1962). Scotus gave as a model the simultaneous unity and distinguishability of the members of the Holy Trinity, a model which had power to silence objectors in his own day but is unfortunately unavailable to me. One model that does seem helpful is the way that the size of a thing stands to its shape. Size and shape are inseparable in particulars, yet they are not related. At the same time they are distinguishable, and particular size and shape vary independently.

There is also one controversial sort of particular which it may be useful to consider here. These are empty spaces or vacua. If we admit them as particulars, then we are certainly able to distinguish between their unrepeatable particularity and their repeatable properties (dimensions, etc.). Yet these aspects are inseparable and far too intimately conjoined to speak of their being related.

It is very difficult, nevertheless, to get rid of the notion that the particularity and the properties of particulars are related constituents of the particular. The matter is taken up by Alan Donagan in his 1963 paper. He remarks that "language inevitably misleads us here" but does not elaborate further. How might language mislead us in this matter?

From the proposition that a has the property, F, we can infer that there exists an object which has F. From 'Fa' we can derive '$(\exists x)$ (Fx)'. It is equally legitimate to infer from the same premiss that there exists a property which a has. From 'Fa' we can derive '$(\exists P)$ (Pa)'. But the symbolism in which these inferences are expressed is potentially misleading. The symbolism of the first inference suggests the doctrine of the particular without its properties, that of the second the doctrine of uninstantiated properties. From this point of view, a different symbolism might be appropriate. From 'Fa' we derive 'F(–)' and also '(–)a'. This symbolism would be awkward in practice, because it makes no provision for the binding of variables. But at least it makes clear that what we are dealing with the whole time is a particular-having-certain-properties.

But even the expression "Fa" is potentially misleading. It is supposed to symbolize a non-relational situation. But it consists of the two expressions "F" and "a" spatially related to each other in a certain manner. The same goes, of course, for attributions of a property in ordinary, non-symbolic, language. This presence of relation at the orthographic–phonetic level, it may then be suggested, generates the illusion of relation at the ontological level.

However, we could conceive of a language where, instead of using predicate-tokens, we simply gave the referring expressions certain properties. For instance, instead of writing "This is green" or "Ga", we could instead write "This" or "*a*" in green ink. Presumably, the systematic use of such a language (supposing this possible) would dispel the illusion of a relation between particulars and their properties.

In speaking of a particular-having-certain-properties I am, of course, simply trying to emphasize the inseparability of particularity and universality. I am not suggesting that 'Fa' is an indivisible semantic unit, in the way that Quine once suggested that 'believes-that-p' is an indivisible semantic unit (1960, p. 216). Obviously, we can and must distinguish between the particularity of a particular, on the one hand, and its properties (and relations), on the other. But it is a distinction without relation.

II *Are there two senses of the word "identity"*?

Pressures towards Nominalism lie deep within every philosopher's mind. This is dramatically illustrated by a last-minute swerve from complete Realism which it is easy to make at this point.

Consider two non-overlapping particulars which have the same property. One might then reason in the following way. Since the two particulars are wholly diverse, they are wholly non-identical in the bed-rock, ultimate, strictest, sense of "identical" ("numerically identical"). Yet is agreed that they have "identical" properties: they are, partially at least, identical in nature. This appears to be a contradiction. It must be resolved by saying that, in the phrase "identical in nature", the word "identical" does not bear the same sense as it does in the phrase "numerically identical". Identity in nature is some milder sort of identity, compatible with complete numerical diversity.

Is this what Scotus had in mind, or at least part of what he had in mind, when he spoke of the *common nature* as a "lesser unity"? Again, is this an element in the moderation of the "moderate" Realism which Scholastic thought upholds against Plato? At any rate, the doctrine that identity of nature is identity in some lesser sense is one which finds countenance in Scholastic thought. Consider, for instance, this quotation from a modern Scholastic:

> the humanity of Peter and the humanity of Paul are distinct but not diverse. The first takes place because there is a lack of real identity between them since the subjects of the "humanity" are two distinct persons; the second occurs because the nature and perfection of "humanity" is totally similar in both Peter and Paul. We can have distinction without diversity although the converse is not true. (Grajewski, 1944, p. 41)

Peter and Paul are not diverse with respect to humanity, yet are not ("really") identical with respect to humanity. Despite a brief flirtation with a Resemblance analysis ("totally similar"), the doctrine here appears to be that identity of nature is a "lesser identity" than numerical identity.

For myself, I cannot understand what this second, lesser, sort of identity is. Partial identity, as when two things overlap but do no more than overlap, or when two things have some but not all the same properties so that their nature "overlaps", can be understood readily enough. But identity is just identity. If there is another, associated, notion we can demand that it receive its own name and that the laws with which it is associated be stated. But I cannot see what this notion could be, nor what laws we could associate with it.

So, faced with the dilemma posed at the beginning of this section, I take it that the Realist ought to allow that two "numerically diverse" particulars which have the same property are *not* wholly diverse. They are partially identical in nature and so are partially identical. That is why I said in the previous section that, for the Realist, the universe is *unified* in a way in which the Nominalist denies that it is unified.

But does not such a doctrine lead to intolerable paradox? For instance, if a and b are both F at a certain time and then b ceases to be F, will not the theory have the consequence that F-ness is destroyed, so that a cannot continue to be F? I believe that all such apparent contradictions can be avoided simply by describing the situation with a little care. If a is F at t_1 and b is F at t_1, but a continues to be F after t_1 while b does not, then a certain partial identity of nature, which held between a and b up to t_1, fails to obtain after t_1. There is no contradiction here. When b ceases to be F, F-ness is not destroyed. Properties are not the sort of thing which can be destroyed (or created). The language of destruction and creation is simply inappropriate in connection with universals. This does not mean that they are eternal Platonic objects. It is helpful here to remember that when particulars are treated as "space-time worms", having an extension in time as well as space, the language of destruction and creation becomes equally inappropriate when applied to them. This does not make particulars into objects immune from destruction!

If all this be a Platonic theory of universals, then I can only say that I think that Plato was right. But as Plato is traditionally interpreted, the theory I am defending is anti-Platonic in at least one respect. There is no separation of particulars and universals.

III *States of affairs*

Universals are nothing without particulars. Particulars are nothing without universals. These theses yield us two Principles, the Principle of Instantiation and the Principle of the Rejection of Bare Particulars. The latter has a Weak and a Strong form.

(1) *The Principle of Instantiation*:
   For each N-adic universal, U, there exist at least N particulars such that they U.

(2) *The Weak Principle of the Rejection of Bare Particulars*:
   For each particular, x, there exists at least one universal, U, such that x is U.

The word 'universal' is deliberately used here because it is neutral between properties and relations.

(2') *The Strong Principle of the Rejection of Bare Particulars*:
   For each particular, x, there exists at least one non-relational property, P, such that x is P.

I wish to assert (2'), but will defer a fuller defence of it until ch. 19 § III.

As already mentioned in ch. 8, a particular's having a property, or two or more particulars standing in some relation, may be called a *state of affairs*. The notion of a state of affairs, however, now requires further discussion. We will concentrate upon the case where a particular has a (non-relational) property.

At this point it is important to notice something which has not been brought out clearly in our previous discussions. There are two conceptions of a particular. We might think of them as the "thick" and the "thin" conceptions respectively. In the first or "thick" conception a particular is a thing taken along with all its properties. But with respect to a particular in this sense we can distinguish between (but not separate) that in virtue of which it is a particular – its particularity – and its non-particular aspects – its properties. This yields us the "thin" conception of a particular. It is a thing taken in abstraction from all its properties.

A state of affairs is defined as a particular's possessing a property or two or more particulars' being related. But we must now ask 'Which of the two conceptions of a particular are we working with in this definition?' It seems that we cannot be working with the first conception. For a particular conceived in the "thick" way is conceived as already possessing its properties. It is, we might say, already a state of affairs. In our notion of a state of affairs, then, we are using the conception of a particular in abstraction from all its properties.

States of affairs seem not too dissimilar from Wittgenstein's *facts*. In the *Tractatus* (1922, 1.1) he said that the world was a world of facts not things. Shall *we* say that the world is a world of states of affairs rather than a world of particulars?

To answer this question we must appeal to our two conceptions of a particular. Given the "thick" conception of a particular it can be said that the world is a world of particulars (though it should be added that the particulars are related to each other). But, as already mentioned two paragraphs ago, particulars in this guise are simultaneously states of affairs. Let me spell out the argument more fully. A conjunction of properties in a particular is itself a property of that particular. (For argument for this, see ch. 15.) The properties of a particular therefore form a single property – the "nature" of that particular. Hence a particular in the "thick" sense is a particular in the "thin" sense possessing a property. Hence it is a state of affairs. So we can say *both* that the world is a world of particulars in the "thick" sense *and* that it is a world of states of affairs. We are saying the same thing in different words. What we must deny is that the world is a world of particulars in the "thin" sense. That, we might say, is the Nominalist conception of the world.

Perhaps, however, the statement that the world is a world of states of affairs requires some qualification. It seems natural to demand that whatever entities we identify as those of which the world is composed should be "substances" in Hume's sense. That is, they should be logically capable of independent existence. Now while it is true that all substances in this sense are states of affairs, it appears not to be true that all states of affairs are substances. For instance, a particular's having a certain property at a certain (mathematical) instant seems to be a state of affairs. But if instants are, as perhaps they are, mere limits of durations, then an instantaneous state of affairs is *not* logically capable of independent existence. Keeping this qualification in mind, however, we can say that the world is a world of states of affairs as well as saying that it is a world of ("thick") particulars.

It may be noted that the notion of a "thick" particular seems to involve its non-relational properties in a way that it does not involve its relations and relational properties. For a particular is a substance, logically capable of independent existence. It could exist although nothing else existed. Suppose, now, that it did exist in this state. It would lack relations and relational properties. For they depend on the existence of the particular together with other particulars. I think that this explains why we think of the non-relational properties of a particular as part of the being of that particular in a way that its relations and relational properties are not.

A very important point now arises. Why do we have these two conceptions of a particular, something which lacks a parallel in our conception of a universal? The answer seems to be this. Consider the state of affairs: particular *a* having the property, F. This state of affairs is not repeatable. It is therefore a particular itself. Particularity taken along with universality yields particularity again. Hence the "thin" and "thick" conceptions of a particular.[1]

So particularity plus universality yields particularity. Let us call this phenomenon "the victory of particularity". It seems to be immensely important for explaining the deep intellectual appeal of Nominalism. It shows why it is so easy to think of particulars as

---

[1] Let us at this point extend our definition of a state of affairs to include *higher-order* particulars, that is universals in so far as they fall under universals. Suppose (as will be argued in Part Seven) that universals can have certain properties and relations. Let it be the case that U_1 has R to U_2. This state of affairs involves nothing but universals. But it is not a universal itself. It cannot be repeated. So it seems to be a particular. It is worth noting, also, that the totality of things – the universe – is a particular.

particulars whether or not we consider them in abstraction from their properties. How easy, in these circumstances, to hold the view that everything is a particular while overlooking that, in the sense in which this is true, the "particulars" involved already enfold universals within themselves!

IV *Particularizing universals*

It is most important to note, however, that although states of affairs are particulars, we can form the notion of a *type* of state of affairs. *a*'s having the property, F, is a state of affairs. But we can form the notion of *something being F* and this is the notion of a *type* of state of affairs.

It might seem that in an ontology such as ours, which does not recognize uninstantiated properties, the distinction between the type of state of affairs *something being F* and the property, F, is a distinction without a difference. Are we not simply taking the universal twice over?

In fact, however, we seem to require the notion of a type of state of affairs. The notion is required in order to elucidate one sort of universal. Consider the predicates '100° centigrade', 'platinum' and 'man'. Let us make the dubious but simplifying assumption that each of these predicates applies in virtue of a single monadic universal. In that case, *being at 100° centigrade* will be a property. It is not quite so clear that the monadic universal, *being platinum*, is a property. This involves problems which will have to be discussed later (ch. 18 § 1), but which are at the moment irrelevant. But what of the predicate 'man'? We are assuming that it applies to particulars in virtue of a single (though obviously not simple) universal. But what (place-holding) name shall we give to this universal? Should it be "humanity"? Does 'man' apply in virtue of the property, *being human*?

This suggestion should make us uneasy. The trouble is that the predicate 'man' is one which, in Quine's phrase, "divides its reference" into individual men. (The corresponding universal may be said to divide its particulars.) The proper characterization of the corresponding universal is not *being human* but rather *being a man*. What this brings out is that there are universals which involve particulars in a quite special way. For *one* man is already a this-such, a particular-having-certain-properties, a state of affairs. It is for universals of this sort that the notion of a *type* of state of affairs is required.

The topic of *particularizing* universals (as we may call them) becomes of great importance where we have complex universals which involve a structure of numerically different parts. For instance, *being a U* might be a matter of *something's being an F* standing in the relation, R, to *something's being a G*. Here the universals U, F and G are all particularizing universals. This becomes especially important to note when we consider that U' might be a matter of *something's being an F* having R to *something else's being an F*. We must reject the notion that this is a matter of the universal, F, standing in any relation to itself. What we have rather is one token of a certain type of state of affairs standing in a certain relation to another token of the very same type.

Particularizing universals have a special link with number. If *being a man* really is a monadic universal (actually a rather improbable assumption), then so is *being (an aggregate of) two men, being (an aggregate of) three men* and so on until the number of men that exist omnitemporally is exhausted. It is clear that the analysis of all these universals involves the notion of a number of different tokens of the same type.

We may further distinguish between universals which particularize strongly and those which only particularize weakly. *Being a man* divides its instantiations into individual men who do not overlap. We may say that it particularizes strongly. Consider, however, *being one kilogram of lead*. If we ask whether or not a certain particular is or is not *one* instance of such a universal, an unambiguous answer can be returned. This contrasts with *being leaden*. If we ignore atoms of lead, a particular which is leaden is at the same time an indefinite number of particulars which are leaden. At the same time, however, *being one kilogram of lead* fails to divide its instantiations into individuals which do not overlap. A large mass of lead contains many overlapping one-kilogram particulars. So we will say that it only particularizes weakly.

So the distinction between token and type, particular and universal, can be drawn for states of affairs, and is required for the conception of a "particularizing" universal. Yet it remains true that the union of particularity and universality found in a state of affairs yields a particular.

v *Particularity and spatio-temporal position*

It is now time to see whether we can carry the question of the nature of particularity (in the "thin" sense) a little further. There is an old line of thought which identifies the particularity of particulars with their spatio-temporal position. (In a useful phrase, suggested by Robert Farrell, instead of speaking of spatio-temporal position we might say "total position".)

a taken four-dimensionally, from the beginning to the end of its existence, occupies a certain spatio-temporal "area", call it p_1t_1. The hypothesis to be examined is that it is occupation of this "area" which constitutes a's particularity.

It might seem easy to make it plausible that the hypothesis is true. For, it might be argued, *being at p_1t_1* is not a universal. If it is a universal, then it must be at least possible that a multiplicity of particulars possess it. But only one particular can have the one total position, so the total position is not a universal. And if *being at p_1t_1* is not a universal, then it is plausible that it constitutes a's particularity. Unfortunately for this argument, however, it is possible for wholly distinct particulars to have the very same (total) position. We shall see this shortly.

But although this argument for saying that *being at p_1t_1* is not a universal fails, it still seems difficult to maintain that it is a universal. We have already noted in ch. 9 § 1, that spatio-temporal positions, considered in abstraction from the sort of things which occupy them, do not appear to differ from each other in any way. A possible case such as the infinite repetition of the universe seems to show that *being at p_1t_1* is neither a non-relational nor a relational property of a. In such a universe, a and its infinite number of counterparts would differ in total position but would *not* differ in nature. The total positions of a and all its counterparts would each have the very same dimensions and "shape".

Tentatively, then, let us see whether it can be maintained that *being at p_1t_1* constitutes the particularity of a. I proceed by considering, and trying to answer, three objections to this hypothesis.

(1) It has often been objected that to explain the numerical difference of two particulars by reference to their (total) positions, simply invites us to explain the numerical difference of the two positions (see, for instance, Russell, 1948, p. 310). The positions,

it seems, can only be *barely* different. But, it is then said, once this point is reached we see that the circuit through positions is unnecessary. We might better have begun simply by saying that the two *particulars* are barely different.

I do not know how to show that this argument is unsound, but I do not think that it can be shown to succeed either. The contention is that bare numerical difference explains the difference of different total positions. But could it not be maintained instead that the so-called "bare" difference of particulars is explained by difference of position? Difference of total position, according to this second line of thought, is not to be explained at all. It constitutes the difference of particulars.

(2) It is at least logically possible that there should be different particulars which do not differ in position because they lack position. Orthodox Dualism holds that, although minds have a position in common time, they are not in physical space. This does not seem to be a self-contradictory hypothesis. What constitutes the numerical distinctness of two Cartesian minds existing at the same time? By hypothesis, it cannot be difference in spatial position. It may be noted further that, once we have rejected the necessity of the Identity of Indiscernibles, their distinctness need not be a matter of different properties either. It is an intelligible supposition that two such co-existing minds might have exactly the same properties, relational as well as non-relational.

Consider also the beloved "private" visual and tactual spaces of the sense-datum theorists. Within a particular private visual field, colour-patches can be differentiated by different position in the field. But what differentiates A's private visual field from a co-existing private visual field of B's? It is not difference of position in physical space: the two visual fields are not, for instance, inside A's and B's heads.

We have already noted Broad's suggestion that it is logically possible for there to be two or more space-times, which might be identical in nature (ch. 9 § 1). Such space-times would be numerically distinct, but not as a result of difference in spatio-temporal position. Again, there may be particulars, such as angels and God, which are not spatio-temporal at all.

The objection does not rely upon the actual existence of non-spatial minds, "private" sensory spaces, alternative space-times, angelic beings and God. I myself think that there is no reason to postulate any of these things. But if they are possible, the argument runs, the particularity of *a* cannot be identified with its spatio-temporal position.

I think that this argument does prove something important. It proves that the concept of particularity is not the very same concept as the concept of a particular's spatio-temporal position. But that is all that it proves. It leaves open the possibility, which I take to be actual, that spatio-temporal position is a form of particularity. If that is so, and if every particular is, as a matter of fact, spatio-temporal, then spatio-temporal position may be the only form of particularity that in fact there is.

(3) The final difficulty for the identification of the particularity of particulars with their spatio-temporal or total position is that it appears possible for two wholly distinct particulars to occupy the very same total position. In order to present this objection, I must first introduce the notion of an "abstract" particular.

I have already briefly mentioned Hume's technical use of the term "substance", which I propose to follow. It is defined as "whatever is capable of independent existence", where "capable of" means no more than "logically capable of". If it is logically possible that something should exist without anything else existing, then, in terms of this definition, that thing is a substance. For Absolute Idealism there is only one substance, but in a pluralistic philosophy such as that of this work, there are indefinitely many substances. A great proportion of these substances will be very different from what would ordinarily be called substances. I would say that every particular (taken with its properties) is a substance, although this statement may involve an element of definition. (Whether all substances are particulars will be discussed briefly in the next chapter.)

If a substance has parts and phases, then these will also be substances. In such cases it is clearly possible to "slice up" substances into spatial and temporal parts in many different, overlapping, ways. But there is another dimension, as it were, a dimension of a non-spatial and non-temporal nature, along which substances can be sliced into further substances, which latter can be said to be parts of the original substance.

Consider, for instance, a coloured cube. It has both visual and tactual properties. Let us assume for the sake of the argument the hypothesis of epistemological realism, that the visual and tactual properties are perceiver-independent, non-relational properties of the cube. Let us also assume that the visual and the tactual properties are completely distinct properties from each other. It is easily conceivable that the cube should lose all its visual qualities, becoming invisible, but retain all its tactual properties such as weight, hardness and temperature. It is also conceivable, not quite so easily but certainly conceivable, that the cube should lose all its tactual properties and become a purely visual (but objectively existing) object having exactly the same visual properties as before the change. Now the original coloured cube was a substance, and the "tactual cube" and the "visual cube" are both substances. Furthermore, there is a clear sense in which the full cube is made up of, has as parts, the tactual and the visual cube. There may be other, overlapping, ways in which the original cube can be "sliced up" into such parts.

I shall call the original coloured cube a *concrete* particular. The tactual and the visual cubes I shall call *abstract* particulars. As already noted, the phrase is that used by some Particularists about properties and relations (ch. 8). But they try to make particulars out of the properties and relations of particulars. My abstract particulars are things which have (universal) properties and relations. It is awkward to use a term already employed by another theory in another sense, but the word "abstract" is appropriate and I can find no better term.

I can now finally come to the point of the third objection to treating the spatio-temporal position of particulars as constituting their particularity. While it is true that only one *concrete* particular can have the one total position, *this does not hold for abstract particulars*. Two different particulars, for instance, the "tactual cube" and the "visual cube", could have exactly the same total position. How, then, it may be asked, can spatio-temporal or total position constitute the particularity of a particular?

Before embarking on an attempt to answer this third objection, it may be noted that, if abstract particulars are possible, it is not a necessary truth that two things cannot be in the same place at the same time. It is only a necessary truth if it is restricted to concrete particulars. It does seem, however, that two particulars, even if abstract, cannot have the same total position if they have the same properties. For how then could they be distinguished from just one particular?

VI *Particularity and spatio-temporal position (continued)*

The third objection which we have just been dealing with is not really very hard to answer, once we have cleared up our minds upon certain points. I proceed by calling attention to five propositions:[1]

> (1) For all particulars, x and y, and total positions, P and Q; if x has P and y has Q and P ≠ Q, then x ≠ y.

This proposition says that *different total positions yield different particulars*. It seems clear that it is a necessary truth. Compare it with:

> *(A) For all particulars, x and y, and properties, F and G; if x has F and y has G and F ≠ G, then x ≠ y.

(A) is so far from being necessary that there are innumerable cases when it is false – all those cases where one particular has two or more distinct properties. For (A) to be a necessary truth, F and G would have to be not merely different but incompatible properties. The necessity of (1) would be explained if the total positions P and Q were *incompatible properties*. But we have found at least some reason to believe that particular total positions are not properties. If so, then, *a fortiori*, they are not incompatible properties, and the necessity of (1) must be explained in some other way.

Notice, further, that although (1) is a necessary truth, (2) is not:

> *(2) For all particulars, x and y, and positions, P and Q; if x has P and y has Q and P = Q, then x = y.

We cannot assert that (2) is necessary because of the possibility that *x* and *y* are distinct "abstract" particulars which are parts of the same concrete particular. *Sameness of total position does not guarantee sameness of particulars.*

We may now introduce the notion of a particular's nature. Its nature is simply the totality of its properties. (Spatio-temporal *properties* will be included in this nature. If vacua are particulars,

---

[1] Here, and henceforward, an asterisk will be used to mark principles which are rejected.

they will have properties.) We then find that nature differentiates p articulars in just the same way that position does:

(3) For all particulars, x and y, and natures, M and N; if x has M and y has N and M ≠ N, then x ≠ y.

This is simply a formulation of the Principle of the Indiscernibility of Identicals which, unlike the Identity of Indiscernibles, is not a Principle which is seriously in dispute. The Principle does involve some problems, notably those involving "opaque" contexts of discourse, but there are few who would wish to solve the problems by abandoning the Principle. I am not among those few. *Difference of nature yields different particulars.*

Notice, now, the parallelism between (1) and (3). The parallelism is reinforced if we consider:

*(4) For all particulars, x and y, and natures M and N, if x has M and y has N and M = N, then x = y.

This is the Identity of Indiscernibles, which we have argued is not a necessary truth (even if non-relational properties are included in a particular's nature). This is parallel to (2) which we also argued was not a necessary truth. *Sameness of nature does not guarantee sameness of particulars.*

We now notice, finally, that although (2) and (4) are not necessary truths, putting together (2) and (4) does seem to yield a necessary truth.

(5) For all particulars, x and y, and total positions, P and Q, and natures, M and N; if x has P and has M and y has Q and has N, and P = Q and M = N, then x = y.

Sameness of total position AND sameness of nature do together guarantee sameness of particulars.[1]

It may be helpful to gather the results together:

(1) Different total positions necessitate different particulars
(2) Sameness of total position does *not* necessitate sameness of particulars
(3) Different natures necessitate different particulars

---

[1] *Perhaps* it can be maintained that, against (5), two particulars can both occupy the same total position and have the same nature. But such particulars, to be two, would require some third principle or "dimension" of individuation of which we know nothing.

(4) Sameness of nature does *not* necessitate sameness of particulars

but

(5) Sameness of total position *and* sameness of nature necessi-
tates sameness of particulars.

(1) and (3) are fairly uncontroversial. (2) and (4) we have had to
argue for. (5) seems plausible.

I believe that we are now in a position to substantiate, though not
actually to prove, the suggestion that spatio-temporal or total
position does, as a matter of fact, constitute the particularity of
particulars (at least for all those particulars which are spatio-
temporal in nature, which in my view are all the particulars that
there are).

Proposition (5) appears to entail that each spatio-temporal particular, concrete or abstract, is some sort of unity of its properties
(its properties include its spatio-temporal *properties*) and its total
position. Between a nature thus conceived, and its total position, we
appear to be able to make only Scotus' "formal distinction". It is not
easy to identify the total position with any further *property*, relational or non-relational, of the particular. So spatio-temporal or
total position appears to constitute the particularity of spatio-
temporal particulars. By adding this particularity to a thing's nature,
or properties, we gain *a particular*: the 'victory of particularity' to
which attention has already been drawn in § III. If spatio-temporal
position had been a property, adding it would simply have augmented the thing's nature, and nature by itself is repeatable, i.e. it
does not by itself constitute a particular.

The fact that different ("abstract") particulars might all have the
same position merely shows that the particularity of a particular
does not completely determine that particular. For such a complete
determination, we also require its nature. This is no more than the
doctrine of the this-such.

What if there are non-spatio-temporal particulars? Some have
held that, for such particulars, they are wholly determined by their
nature. Aquinas held to this doctrine in the case of angels, asserting
that sameness of nature by itself entailed sameness of angel (*Summa
Theologica*, Part I, Q. 50, Art. 4). But, in agreement with Scotus
(*Ordinatio*, II, Dist. 3, pars I, Q. 7), I see no reason to accept this
view. The conception of indiscernible angels appears to be an intelli-

gible conception, while the conception of angels as universals appears to be a dubious one. I suggest that such non-spatio-temporal beings would have an unknown principle of particularity between which, and their nature, only a formal distinction could be made.

A little more remains to be said about particulars and spatio-temporal position. But this I will defer until ch. 18 § 1.

12

A world-hypothesis[1]

Here are three world-hypotheses in decreasing order of generality.
(1) The world contains nothing but particulars having properties
and related to each other. (2) The world is nothing but a single
spatio-temporal system. (3) The world is completely described in
terms of (completed) physics. I put forward the view that each of
these propositions is true. Notice that although (2) is less general
than (1), and (3) less general than (2), the propositions seem to be
logically independent. (Though it would be strange to accept (3)
and deny (2).) Nor do I suggest that there is any particular epistemological order of priority among the hypotheses; although (3)
seems the most dubious.

Hypothesis (1) is clearly a hypothesis of "first philosophy":
one could hardly put forward a more general hypothesis than this. I
shall understand it as asserting that properties and relations are
universals, that particulars are not to be wholly analysed in terms of
universals, but that the particularity of particulars is not a substratum standing in a certain relation to its properties and relations.
Such a doctrine is a Realism, but is an anti-Platonic Realism. In a
broad sense, it is an Aristotelian Realism. It is however a *minimal*
Realism, because it admits nothing in the world but particulars,
their properties and their relations. I shall, however, allow one
expansion of this minimal Realism. In Part Seven it will be argued
that these properties and relations can themselves have certain properties and be related to each other in certain ways. (It will be argued
further that causality is to be explained in terms of such higher-
order relations.)

The object of this chapter is not to defend the positive conten-
tions of this version of Realism. That is the task of the previous
chapters together with the next volume. In this chapter my concern
will be to argue that we have no reason to postulate anything over

---

[1]Much of the material in this chapter is also to be found in Armstrong (1978), where
more is said in defence of (3), in particular.

and above particulars, their properties and their relations (together with certain higher-order properties and relations). My concern will be to criticize the view that we require to postulate any further sorts of entity than these.

Before I embark upon this task, however, a word about hypotheses (2) and (3).

In the previous chapter it was suggested that spatio-temporal or "total" position does, as a matter of fact not of logic, constitute the particularity of spatio-temporal particulars. Nevertheless, (2), although a hypothesis of great generality, seems not to be a hypothesis of first philosophy. (It may be called the hypothesis of "Naturalism".) To accept Naturalism is to reject such entities as Cartesian minds, private visual and tactual spaces, angelic beings and God. (It need not exclude the notion that the spatio-temporal nature of things is analysable and explicable in terms of some more deeply hidden physical features.) Some of these entities, or some ways of conceiving of these entities, involve logical difficulties. But for the most part, I conceive, the fundamental objections to postulating these entities are scientific and even observational. Following D. C. Williams (1963, p. 74), we may distinguish between 'analytic ontology' and 'speculative cosmology'. (1) is a thesis of analytic ontology, i.e., first philosophy, the direct concern of this work; (2) and (3), by comparison, are simply theses of 'speculative cosmology'.

(3) is the hypothesis of modern Reductive Materialism or Physicalism. The complete "supremacy of physics" which it argues for is a somewhat open-ended notion and the hypothesis is to that extent vague. But I believe that we can specify circumstances in which, although (2) was accepted, (3) would have to be given up. An instance would be the correctness of the biological hypothesis of Vitalism. (3) is very definitely a scientific hypothesis (or "research programme"), though at a high level of generality. The chief service which philosophy can render to (3) is to show that the *a priori* or relatively *a priori* objections which many philosophers make to it are not weighty. (3) will not be defended in this work, although I am prepared to defend it and have defended it elsewhere.

Let us return, then, to considering (1), the hypothesis that the world contains nothing but propertied particulars related to each other. This minimal Realism is a less economical view than the Nominalist world-hypothesis, *viz.* that the world is simply a world of particulars which are nothing but particulars. Nevertheless, (1) is still a very economical hypothesis, and many philosophers have thought that the types of entities which it postulates are too few by themselves to give a satisfactory account of all phenomena.

A bewildering variety of additional entities have been deemed necessary by some philosophers. There have been postulations of transcendent universals, a realm of numbers, transcendent standards of value, timeless propositions, non-existent objects such as the golden mountain, *possibilia* and/or possible worlds, "abstract" classes which are something more than the aggregate of their members, including unit-classes and the null-class. Of course, not every philosopher who has postulated additional entities has postulated this whole set, and sometimes some of the postulations have been designed to avoid commitment to properties and relations, so that there are some "trade-offs" in economy.

However, despite the diversity of these postulations, and the diversity of the reasons given for them, it seems that an upholder of (1), our moderate but minimal Realism, can advance a single, very powerful, line of argument which is a difficulty for them all. The argument takes the form of a dilemma. Are these entities capable of *acting upon particulars*, or are they not? As the argument is developed, it will turn out to be a defence of (2), the hypothesis of Naturalism, also.

In the *Phaedo* (95–106) Plato endowed his Forms with causal power. They act upon particulars, giving the latter their nature, to the extent that they have a nature. Karl Popper's recently postulated "third world" of conjectures appears to be a realm of *propositions*, the meanings of sentences (Popper, 1973). His "third world" interacts causally with the "second world" of mind, which in turn interacts with the material world. A similar position was held by Frege (1918–19), although his "third realm" acts upon, but is not acted upon by, the mind. However, despite the exceptions which Plato, Frege and Popper represent, the diverse entities postulated are not normally thought to act upon particulars.

Indeed, there are great difficulties in conceiving that such entities do act upon particulars. First, there are logical or conceptual difficulties. None of these extra entities is taken ever to change. In typical cases of causation, however, one change brings about another. It follows, then, that if these entities act upon particulars, they do not act in this typical way. How, then, do they work? Could they be conceived as sustaining particulars in a certain state,

or as exerting some sort of steady, unchanging, pressure upon particulars which, in certain circumstances, gives rise to certain effects?
Such a notion is perhaps barely possible, but it is impossible to see
how such alleged causal operation could ever be identified. For
instance, when sustaining causes are postulated *in nature*, the postulations can be tested by observing situations where the alleged
sustaining cause is absent. If the alleged effect is also absent, the
hypothesis is supported. But no such verification is possible, even in
principle, in the case of unchanging entities.

But even if these difficulties could be overcome, and the logical
possibility of causal influence upon particulars by these entities
established, the development of the natural sciences suggests that the
logical possibility is no more than a logical possibility. Consider
again the Naturalist hypothesis (2), that the world is nothing but a
single spatio-temporal system. Whether or not this is true, at least
the positive part of it is true, for there certainly is a spatio-temporal
system of particulars.[1] Call it "Nature". Whether there is anything
else than Nature must be admitted to be controversial. Furthermore,
we have fairly good scientific reasons to believe that Nature, the
spatio-temporal system, is a causally self-enclosed system.

This view has not been held in the past. For instance, religious
thinkers often used to think of God as outside but intervening
freely in Nature. He might give victory to the righteous or answer
prayers for rain in defiance of the way that matters would have
shaped if Nature had been left to its own devices. But those who still
believe in a transcendent God are increasingly reluctant to believe
that he acts upon Nature in this way. They may hold that God
created Nature, and created it for a purpose which is still working
itself out. But they are likely to believe that he does not intervene.

Consider, again, the Dualist or non-spatial theory of the mind.
Descartes saw clearly that, if Dualist *Interactionism* (as opposed to
Parallelism) was to be made plausible, then he must postulate
places in the brain where physical events occur whose immediate
causes are, in part at least, spiritual happenings. He guessed that this
happened in the pineal gland, but we now know that this gland can
play no such role. Where, then, do spiritual happenings have their
immediate physical effects? No plausible suggestion has been made.
The neurophysiological evidence suggests that what happens to the

---

[1] Phenomenalism and Absolute Idealism deny this, in any but Pickwickian senses.
Here I simply assume that they are false.

brain has no other cause except earlier states of the brain and its physical environment.

Yet the cases of God and the soul are the two most plausible cases of things outside Nature acting upon it. If the case for God and the soul acting upon particulars is weak, it is far weaker in the case of the realm of numbers, possible words, propositions and so on. Suppose, for instance, that there is a transcendent realm of numbers. How implausible to think that this realm, or some selected portion of it, can act upon a central nervous system.

So let us now explore the other horn of the dilemma. Let us assert that none of these postulated entities acts upon Nature in any way. This remedy, I maintain, is worse than the disease.

The argument is this. A spatio-temporal realm of particulars certainly exists (it includes our bodies). Whether anything else exists is controversial. If any entities outside this realm are postulated, but it is stipulated further that they have no manner of causal action upon the particulars in this realm, then there is no compelling reason to postulate them. Occam's razor then enjoins us not to postulate them.

Natural science has made spectacular advances as a result of positing unobserved entities. Consider microbes, genes, atoms, molecules, electrons, quarks and black holes. The fruitfulness of such posits is a standing reproach to any Positivistic conception of natural science. Contemporary analytic philosophers are deeply affected by the justified reaction against Positivism. It has become fashionable, therefore, to compare the positing of transcendent entities in first philosophy with the positing of theoretical entities in natural science, entities of the sort just mentioned. Here is George Berry (1968, p. 233):

How then do we find out about this realm of extra-mental, non-particular, unobservable entities? Our knowledge of them, like our knowledge of the extra-mental, unobservable objects of the physical sciences, is indirect, being tied to perceived things by a fragile web of theory. In both cases – physics and logic – our hypotheses about the unperceived are tested by their success in accounting for the character of the perceived. Misreading this similarity, one might easily conclude that a faculty of non-sensory perception, call it 'intuition' is necessary to play a part in logic parallel to the role of sensation in physics. The conclusion is groundless. Long-run success in dealing with the same old perceptual field of ordinary sensation holistically confirms not only our belief in a force satisfying an inverse-square law but also, if more remotely, our belief in the derivations used to compute the force. It also confirms our belief in the classes ultimately invoked to so analyze the derivatives as to explain the computations.

In fact, however, there is a vital difference between the unobserved entities of science and the philosopher's postulations, which Berry overlooks. The abstract classes which he favours may serve as truth-conditions for those propositions of mathematics required for physics. But, as Berry would presumably admit, they do not *bring about* anything in the realm of Nature in the way that genes and electrons do. Genes and electrons have causal efficacy. Abstract classes do not. In what way, then, can the latter help to explain the properties and behaviour of spatio-temporal particulars? Physics requires the truth of mathematics. That is not in dispute. But must it not be possible to give an explanation of the truth-conditions of mathematical statements in some way or other which does not appeal to entities outside Nature which can have no influence on particulars?

Consider as a parallel the position of an upholder of the Representative theory of perception. He agrees with the Phenomenalists that the only immediate knowledge yielded by perception is knowledge of the occurrence of sense-data. But he wishes to maintain against the Phenomenalist that there are physical objects lying beyond the data. He cannot observe these objects directly, but claims that it is reasonable to postulate them. If asked to justify his postulation, he will naturally appeal to the causal role which such objects are supposed to play. If there are continuing and interacting physical objects acting upon our physical sense-organs and, as a result, bringing sense-data into existence, then we can explain in a general way the particular trains of sense-data which each individual perceiver senses.

But now suppose that physical objects are still postulated, but that physical objects are given no power to cause sense-data. The Phenomenalist case now seems to be unanswerable, and the Representationalist cause lost. The hypothesis of the physical realm becomes a quite idle one. Why should our ontology find a place for such a drone? And if our actually used physical-object expressions are thought to have referents, then these referents can only be the sense-data themselves.

Should not exactly the same line of reasoning apply to other causally idle entities?

So, given a world of particulars having properties and standing in relations, a world which is a spatio-temporal world, there seem to be good scientific, as well as conceptual, reasons for treating it as causally self-contained, not acted upon by other sorts of entity. And if these other sorts of entity do not act upon this world of particulars, then there seems to be no methodological reason for postulating them.

There is no doubt that accepting this argument leaves the upholder of (minimal) Realism with a problem. He is committed to giving an account of possibilities, of propositions, of numbers, of classes, etc. within the framework of his relatively exiguous ontology. (It is, however, much richer than the Nominalist's ontology.) Nor does anything which has been said here give any particular hint how the job should be done. All the argument of this chapter can do is to give us confidence that, somehow, the job can be done. It gives us confidence to pursue a certain research-programme.

Arising out of the discussion of this chapter we can now say a further brief word about the fundamental notion of a particular. I have not attempted to define the notion up to this point, and it may not be possible in any case. I have said that (propertied) particulars are substances and that their parts and phases are substances, meaning by "a substance" what is logically capable of independent existence. A collection of particulars (scattered or not) will also be a particular, and so a substance. If the world consists simply of particulars having properties and relations, then we can say not only that all particulars are substances, but also that all substances are particulars.

To this we can add: if the world consists simply of particulars having properties and relations, it is particulars and particulars alone which can act and be acted upon. But we must add: they act and are acted on solely in virtue of their properties, non-relational and relational; in virtue of their nature. Another way of putting this is that it is states of affairs which are causes. It is often said that it is events which are really causes. But events seem to be, or at least to be analysable in terms of, states of affairs as we have defined them.

The argument of Volume II

Volume II is divided into four Parts. In the first Part, *Predicates and Universals*, it is argued that predicates (predicate-types) are correlated with universals in a many–many rather than a one–one manner. Given a predicate applying to certain particulars, it may apply in virtue of many, one or no universals. Given a universal there may be many, one or no predicates corresponding to it. It is the mistaken identification of universals with meanings, the meanings of predicates, which has prevented the realization that no simple correlation of predicates and universals can be found.

It is argued in particular that if 'P' and 'Q' are distinct predicates, each applying in virtue of genuine universals, then 'P∨Q', '∼P' and '∼Q' do not so apply. There are no disjunctive or negative universals. It is argued, however, that provided there is a particular to which both 'P' and 'Q' apply, then there is a universal, P&Q. There are conjunctive universals. P and Q are proper parts of this conjunctive universal.

But how is it determined when we have arrived at genuine generic identities, genuine universals? It is argued that we have nowhere to begin but with the classifications which we naturally make. Natural science may then take us beyond these classifications to more deeply hidden classings and sortings which, it is our hope, approach more closely to an isolation of genuine universals. Formal identity criteria for universals may be given. They are identical if and only if they bestow identical causal powers upon the particulars which fall under them. But the *identification* of universals must be *a posteriori*.

In the final chapter of the first Part, it is argued that non-synonymous predicates may apply to the very same particulars in virtue of the very same universals. Such predicates may stand to such universals in different fashions. Predicates may be said to "name", to "analyse" or else to be "external" to the universals. All this casts light upon the nature of the so-called "contingent identification of properties", for example, colour with light-waves and mental states with physical states of the brain.

The second Part of the volume, *Properties and Relations*, tries to advance first the theory of properties, and then the theory of relations, in a more direct manner. In the chapter on properties it is denied, *pace* Aristotle, that we need to recognize special sorts of monadic universals associated with stuffs and kinds (*being gold* and *being an electron*). An account of such universals can be given in terms of instantiated conjunctions of properties, and an instantiated conjunction of properties is a property.

A classification of various categories of property is then made, including the important category of *structural* property. The properties (and relations) which go to make up a structural property do *not* qualify the very same particular which the structural property qualifies, but, rather, proper parts of that particular. In ch. 18 § v it is suggested that the "foundation in things" for the notion of *number* lies in non-relationally structural properties possessed by the particular which is the aggregate (not the class) of the things numbered.

In ch. 19 it is first argued that we do not need to recognize relational properties as anything over and above (non-relational) properties and relations. The question is then taken up whether *all* properties may not dissolve *ad infinitum* into structures of propertied-things-in-relation, so that there are no *irreducible* properties. It is concluded that this is possible, although it does not have to be so. The familiar distinction between internal and external relations is then drawn. It is argued that internal relations are reducible to properties of the "related" things. It is then tentatively suggested that all genuine (i.e. external) relations holding between first-order particulars are spatio-temporal relations. Finally, it is argued that particulars are never reflexively related. Any relation must relate at least two distinct particulars.

The third Part of volume II, *The Analysis of Resemblance*, tries to give an account of various sorts of resemblance. The resemblance of particulars involves no especial difficulties. It is a matter of the resembling things' having certain properties. But certain cases of the "resemblance of universals", for example that of the lengths among themselves and the colours among themselves, raise great difficulties. Difficulties are found in various projects: to reduce such resemblances to the resemblance of (first-order) particulars; to account for the resemblances in terms of common properties or relations of the universals involved (second-order properties and relations); to account for the resemblances by drawing the distinction between determinable and determinate properties; and, finally, in the attempt to give a subjectivist account of such resemblances.

It is then argued that there are no determinable universals, only determinates. The problem arises, what unifies classes of universals such as the determinate lengths or the determinate shades of colour. It is suggested that the unifying factor is a series of *partial identities* holding between different members of the class in question. The conjunctive properties P&Q and Q&R are partially identical. But in the case of the lengths, colours, etc., it is argued that the properties involved are *structural* properties. Hence the partial identities concerned are identities of parts of such structures. This solution can be rather easily applied to the case of the lengths. But it meets *epistemological* difficulties in the case of the colours, which appear to be simple and unstructured. It is suggested that the colours are in fact structural properties, although we are unable to perceive this structure.

In the fourth and final Part of volume II, *Higher-order Universals*, it is argued that there are second-order (and perhaps higher-order) universals: properties and relations of properties and relations. But a thesis of *Formalism* is upheld. It is suggested that higher-order universals are restricted to formal or topic-neutral universals, such universals as *being complex* as opposed to *being a colour*.

The investigation of higher-order properties is of rather a tentative sort. In the case of higher-order relations, it is suggested that these are restricted to the relations between universals of (non-logical) *necessitation, probabilification* and *exclusion*. It is further suggested that these relations constitute *the laws of nature*. A law of nature, on this view, is something more than a mere uniformity in nature. It is a uniformity springing from a relation holding between the *universals* involved. In this way, it is suggested, a Realism about universals is able to give a non-sceptical answer to the problem of what constitutes a law of nature. *Causal* connection is seen as a particular case of nomic connection.

Glossary of terms used and principles formulated

(Principles and notions rejected are *starred.*)

Abstract particulars. Particulars of which there can be more than one at the same place and time; also (*) properties and relations as particulars (Stout).

A posteriori Realism. The doctrine that what universals there are has to be established *a posteriori*, on the basis of total science.

**A priori Realism.* The doctrine that what universals there are can be established *a priori*, for instance on the basis of meanings.

**Argument from Meaning.* Argument to universals from the meanings of predicates.

Aristotelian Realism. Immanent Realism (*q.v.*).

**Bare particulars.* Particulars which lack properties, or which lack both properties and relations (see Bare particulars, rejection of, the Weak and Strong Principles).

Bare particulars, rejection of, the Strong Principle. For each particular, *x*, there exists at least one non-relational property, P, such that *x* is P.

Bare particulars, rejection of, the Weak Principle. For each particular, *x*, there exists at least one universal, U, such that *x* is U.

**Bit theory.* See Mereological Nominalism.

**Bundle theory of particulars.* The doctrine that a particular is nothing but a "bundle" of properties conceived of as universals (see Universalism).

**Cases.* Properties and relations as particulars (Wolterstorff).

**Class Nominalism.* The reductive doctrine that for particulars to have the same property, or to have the same relation, is for them to be members of the same class of particulars.

**Complete complex of compresence.* A class of (universal) properties such that each member of the class is compresent with each other member of the class, and there is no property compresent with each member of the class which is not a member of the class. Used by Russell as the definition of a particular.

Compresence. Primitive relation holding between any two members of the class of properties which, on a Bundle theory of particulars (*q.v.*), go to make a particular.

Concept Nominalism. The reductive doctrine that for particulars to have the same property, or to have the same relation, is for them to fall under the same concept.

Concrete particulars. Particulars such that no two can occupy the very same places and times.

Dissimilarity of the Diverse. McTaggart's term for the Identity of Indiscernibles (*q.v.*).

Distributive unity. Form of unity postulated by Stout to obtain between all those particularized properties and relations which have the same (universal) property or relation.

Equality. Relation said to hold between particularized properties and relations which are of the same kind, e.g. by G. Küng.

Formal distinction. The non-relational distinction which Scotus holds can be drawn between the haecceity (*q.v.*) and the nature of a particular.

Haecceity. Scotus' term for the particularity, or thisness, of particulars.

Higher-order particulars. Properties and relations considered as having properties and relations.

Higher-order universals. Properties and relations of properties and relations.

Identity of Indiscernibles. The view that different particulars cannot have all the same properties. In the *Strong* form of the doctrine the properties are confined to non-relational properties; in the *Weak* form all properties are included.

Identity view. The view that properties and relations are universals.

Immanent Realism. The doctrine which admits universals but denies that they are transcendent.

Indiscernibility of Identicals. If *a* and *b* are the very same particular, then any property is a property of *a* if and only if it is a property of *b*.

Inherence. Converse of the relation of *support* (*q.v.*).

Instantiation, Principle of. For each *n*-adic universal, U, there exist at least *n* particulars such that they are U.

Lockean view of particulars. The view that particulars involve a substratum *related* to the properties of the particular.

Materialism, Reductive. The doctrine that the concepts and laws of physics are sufficient to give a complete account of the nature of things.

*Mereological Nominalism. The reductive doctrine that for particulars to have the same property, or to have the same relation, is for them to be parts of the same aggregate of particulars.

Naturalism. The hypothesis that nothing but Nature, the single, all-embracing spatio-temporal system, exists.

Nature. The single, all-embracing spatio-temporal system.

Nature of a particular. The complete conjunction of a particular's properties, itself a property.

*Nominalism. The doctrine that whatever exists is a particular, and nothing but a particular.

Non-Identity assumption. The assumption that a Form cannot participate in itself.

Objectivist theories of properties and relations. Any doctrine which gives an account of the properties and relations of particulars as existing independently of the relation of the particulars to minds or systems of classification.

Object regress. Attempts to criticize Relational analyses (*q.v.*) by showing that the entities appealed to by such analyses themselves require the very same analysis.

One over Many argument. The argument to universals from the apparent existence of identities of nature between different particulars.

*Participation. Relation which it was suggested that particulars have to Forms.

*Particularism. The doctrine that the properties and relations of particulars are themselves (first-order) particulars.

*Particularized qualities. Qualities as particulars (Strawson).

Particularizing universals. Universals which yield an unambiguous answer to the question whether or not a particular is *one* instance of that universal. If the universal "divides its instantiations", yielding nothing but discrete, non-overlapping particulars, then it particularizes *strongly*. If not, it particularizes *weakly*.

*Perfect particulars. Properties and relations as particulars (Bergmann).

*Platonic Realism. See Transcendent Realism.

*Predicate Nominalism. The reductive doctrine that for particulars to have

the same property, or have the same relation, is for the same predicate to apply to them.

Predicates, identity-conditions for. Predicate-tokens are of identical type iᴚ and only if they are synonymous.

*Property-instances. Properties as particulars.

Propositional predicate. The predicate of a proposition (as opposed to a sentence).

Realism. The doctrine that there are universals.

*Relational analysis. Any doctrine which gives a reductive account of a particular's having properties or relations in terms of further *relations* between the particular and some further entity or entities.

*Relational Immanent Realism. The form of Immanent Realism (*q.v.*) which takes the particularity and universality of particulars to be *related* constituents of the particulars.

Relation regress. Attempts to criticize Relational analyses (*q.v.*) by show-ing that the relations appealed to by such analyses themselves require the same analysis.

*Resemblance Nominalism. The reductive doctrine that for particulars to have the same property, or have the same relation, is for them to have a sufficient resemblance to some paradigm particular(s).

Restricted Third Man. A particular case of Plato's Third Man argument (*q.v.*).

Scientific Realism (about universals). See *A posteriori* Realism.

*Self-predication assumption. The view that the Form of F-ness must itself be an F.

*Singularist theory of causation. The view that in a causal sequence it is a particular *qua* particular which acts to bring about its effect.

State of affairs. A particular (including higher-order particulars) having a property, or two or more particulars being related.

*Stoutian particulars. Properties and relations as particulars.

*Subjectivist theories of properties and relations. Any doctrine which gives an account of the properties and relations of particulars in terms of the relation of the particulars to systems of classification and/or minds.

Substance, Hume's definition of. Whatever is logically capable of inde-pendent existence.

*Substratum. The particularity of particulars conceived of as *related* to the

properties and relations of the particulars (see Relational Immanent Realism).

*Support. Relation supposed to obtain between substrata and properties in the Relational form of Immanent Realism (*q.v.*).

Third Bed argument. Plato's "argument" to show that Forms are essentially unique.

*Third Man argument. Plato's argument to show that the theory of Forms is involved in an infinite regress.

Tie. The non-relational connection between particularity and universality argued for by the non-relational form of Immanent Realism (*q.v.*).

Total position. The spatio-temporal area occupied by a particular from the beginning to the end (if any) of its existence.

*Transcendent Realism. The doctrine that universals exist separated from particulars.

*Tropes. Properties and relations as particulars (Williams).

*Unit Properties. Properties and relations as particulars (Matthews and Cohen).

*Universalism. The doctrine that whatever exists is a universal, and nothing but a universal (see Bundle theory of particulars).

Victory of particularity. The fact that the "union" of particularity and universality yields a particular, not a universal.

Works cited

Aaron, R. I. (1939) Two Senses of the Word *Universal*, *Mind*, 68

Anderson, J. (1962) *Studies in Empirical Philosophy*, Angus and Robertson

Anscombe, G. E. M. (1971) Causality and Determination, Inaugural Lecture, Cambridge University Press

Aquinas, St. T. *Summa Theologica*, 3 vols., trans. by the Dominican Fathers, Benziger Brothers 1947–8

Armstrong, D. M. (1973) *Belief, Truth and Knowledge*, Cambridge University Press

Armstrong, D. M. (1974) Infinite Regress Arguments and the Problem of Universals, *Australasian Journal of Philosophy*, 52

Armstrong, D. M. (1975) Towards a Theory of Properties, *Philosophy*, 50

Armstrong, D. M. (1978) Naturalism, Materialism and First Philosophy, *Philosophia*

Ayer, A. J. (1954) *Philosophical Essays*, Macmillan

Ayer, A. J. (1971) *Russell and Moore: The Analytical Heritage*, Macmillan

Barnett, D. (1974) A New Semantical Theory of Egocentric Particulars, *Synthese*, 28

Bergmann, G. (1964) *Logic and Reality*, University of Wisconsin Press

Bergmann, G. (1967) *Realism*, University of Wisconsin Press

Berkeley, G. *Principles of Human Knowledge*, in *Berkeley's Philosophical Writings*, ed. Armstrong, D. M., Collier-Macmillan 1965

Berkeley, G. *Three Dialogues between Hylas and Philonous* in *Berkeley's Philosophical Writings*, ed. Armstrong, D. M., Collier-Macmillan 1965

Berry, G. (1968) Logic with Platonism, *Synthese*, 19

Black, M. (1952) The Identity of Indiscernibles, *Mind*, 61, reprinted with additional notes in Black, M., *Problems of Analysis*, Routledge 1954

Black, M. (1971) The Elusiveness of Sets, *The Review of Metaphysics*, 24

Blanshard, B. (1939) *The Nature of Thought*, Allen and Unwin

Blanshard, B. (1962) *Reason and Analysis*, Open Court

Bochenski, I. M. (1956) The Problem of Universals, in *The Problem of Universals*, Notre Dame University Press

Boler, J. F. (1963) *Charles Peirce and Scholastic Realism*, University of Washington Press

Bradley, F. H. (1897) *Appearance and Reality*, 2nd ed., Oxford University Press

Brandt, R. B. (1957) The Languages of Realism and Nominalism, *Philosophy and Phenomenological Research*, 17

Broad, C. D. (1933) *Examination of McTaggart's Philosophy*, vol. 1, Cambridge University Press

142 *Works cited*

Brownstein, D. (1973) *Aspects of the Problem of Universals*, The University of Kansas

Carnap, R. (1967) *The Logical Structure of the World*, trans. George, R. A., Routledge

Chakrabarti, K. (1975) The Nyāya-Vaiśeṣika Theory of Universals, *Journal of Indian Philosophy*, 3

Clarke, F. P. (1962) St. Thomas on "Universals", *The Journal of Philosophy*, 59

Cook Wilson, J. (1926) *Statement and Inference*, 2 vols., Oxford University Press

Cresswell, M. J. (1975) What is Aristotle's Theory of Universals? *Australasian Journal of Philosophy*, 53

Davidson, D. (1965) Theories of Meaning and Learnable Languages, in *Logic, Methodology and Philosophy of Science*, Proceedings of the 1964 International Congress, ed. Bar-Hillel, Y., North Holland

Demos, R. (1946) A Note on Plato's Theory of Ideas, *Philosophy and Phenomenological Research*, 8

Donagan, A. (1963) Universals and Metaphysical Realism, *The Monist*, 47

Duncan-Jones, A. E. (1934) Universals and Particulars, *Proceedings of the Aristotelian Society*, 34

Frege, G. (1918–19) The Thought: A Logical Inquiry, translated A. M. and Marcelle Quinton, *Mind*, 65, 1956, reprinted in *Philosophical Logic*, ed. Strawson, P. F., Oxford University Press 1967

Goodman, N. (1956) A World of Individuals, in *The Problem of Universals*, Notre Dame University Press, reprinted with Appendix, in Goodman, N., *Problems and Projects*, Bobbs-Merrill 1972

Goodman, N. (1966) *The Structure of Appearance*, 2nd ed., Bobbs-Merrill

Grajewski, M. J. (1944) *The Formal Distinction of Duns Scotus*, The Catholic University of America Press

Hampshire, S. (1950) Scepticism and Meaning, *Philosophy*, 25

Hochberg, H. (1965) Universals, Particulars and Predication, *The Review of Metaphysics*, 19

Hochberg, H. (1966) Things and Descriptions, *American Philosophical Quarterly*, 3

Hochberg, H. (1969) Moore and Russell on Particulars, Relations and Identity, in *Studies in the Philosophy of G. E. Moore*, ed. Klemke, E. D., Quadrangle books

Hume, D. *A Treatise of Human Nature*, 2 vols., Everyman (1911)

Husserl, E. (1913) *Logical Investigations*, 2nd ed., trans. Findlay, J. N., Routledge 1970

Jackson, F. C. (1977) Statements about Universals, *Mind*, 76

Johnson, W. E. (1921) *Logic, Part I*, Cambridge University Press

Jones, J. R. (1949) Are the Qualities of Particular Things Universal or Particular?, *Philosophical Review*, 58

Jones, J. R. (1951) Characters and Resemblances, *Philosophical Review*, 60

Kemp Smith, N. (1927) The Nature of Universals (III), *Mind*, 36

Kretzmann, N. (1970) Medieval Logicians on the Meaning of the *Propositio*, *Journal of Philosophy*, 67

Küng, G. (1964) Concrete and Abstract Properties, *Notre Dame Journal of Formal Logic*, 5

Küng, G. (1967) *Ontology and the Logistic Analysis of Language*, revised ed., Reidel

Locke, J. *Essay concerning Human Understanding*, 2 vols., Everyman (1961)

Loux, M. J. (1974) Kinds and the Dilemma of Individuation, *The Review of Metaphysics*, 27

Loux, M. J. Identity and Compresence: An Examination of Russell's Later Theory of Substance, (forthcoming)

Mackie, J. L. (1976) *Problems from Locke*, Oxford University Press

McMullin, E. (1958) The Problem of Universals, *Philosophical Studies*, 8

McTaggart, J. McT. E. (1921) *The Nature of Existence*, 2 vols., Cambridge University Press

Matthews, G. B. and Cohen, S. M. (1968) The One and the Many, *Review of Metaphysics*, 21

Mill, J. S. *A System of Logic*, ed. Robson, J. M., University of Toronto Press and Routledge 1973

Moore, G. E. (1953) *Some Main Problems of Philosophy*, Allen and Unwin

Pap, A. (1959) Nominalism, Empiricism and Universals: 1, *Philosophical Quarterly*, 9

Plato, *Parmenides*, trans. Taylor, A. E., Oxford University Press 1934

Plato, *Phaedo*, trans. Gallop, D., Oxford University Press 1975

Plato, *Republic*, trans. Cornford, F. M., Oxford University Press 1941

Popper, K. R. (1973) *Objective Knowledge*, Oxford University Press

Price, H. H. (1953) *Thinking and Experience*, Hutchinson

Putnam, H. (1970a) On Properties, in *Essays in Honour of Carl G. Hempel*, ed. Rescher N., Reidel, reprinted in Putnam, H., *Philosophical Papers*, vol. 1, Cambridge University Press 1975

Quine, W. V. O. (1960) *Word and Object*, M.I.T. Press

Quine, W. V. O. (1966) *The Ways of Paradox*, Random House

Quine, W. V. O. (1969) *Ontological Relativity*, Columbia University Press

Quinton, A. (1957) Properties and Classes, *Proceedings of the Aristotelian Society*, 48

Quinton, A. (1973) *The Nature of Things*, Routledge

Raphael, D. D. (1955) Universals, Resemblance and Identity, *Proceedings of the Aristotelian Society*, 55

Russell, B. (1911) On the Relations of Universals and Particulars, *Proceedings of the Aristotelian Society*, 12, reprinted, with an added paragraph, in *Logic and Knowledge*, ed. Marsh, R. C., Allen and Unwin 1956

Russell, B. (1912) *The Problems of Philosophy*, Home University Library

Russell, B. (1940) *An Inquiry into Meaning and Truth*, Allen and Unwin

Russell, B. (1948) *Human Knowledge, its Scope and Limits*, Allen and Unwin

Russell, B. (1959) *My Philosophical Development*, Allen and Unwin

Ryle, G. (1939) Plato's Parmenides, *Mind*, 48, reprinted in Ryle, G., *Collected Papers*, vol. 1, Hutchinson 1971

Scotus, D. *Opera Omnia*, vol. VIII Civitas Vaticana 1973

Searle, J. R. (1969) *Speech Acts*, Cambridge University Press

Stenius, E. (1974) Sets, *Synthese*, 27

Stout, G. F. (1921) *The Nature of Universals and Propositions*, Oxford University Press (British Academy Lecture), reprinted in Stout, G. F., *Studies in Philosophy and Psychology*, Macmillan 1930

Stout, G. F. (1923) Are the characteristics of particular things universal or particular?, *Proceedings of the Aristotelian Society*, supp. vol. 3

Stout, G. F. (1936) Universals again, *Proceedings of the Aristotelian Society*, supp. vol. 15

Strawson, P. F. (1959) *Individuals*, Methuen

Strawson, P. F. (1974) *Subject and Predicate in Logic and Grammar*, Methuen

Weinberg, S. (1974) Unified Theories of Elementary-Particle Interaction, *Scientific American*, 231

Williams, D. C. (1953) The Elements of Being, *The Review of Metaphysics*, 6, reprinted in Williams, D.C., *Principles of Empirical Realism*, Charles Thomas 1966

Williams, D. C. (1963) Necessary Facts, *The Review of Metaphysics*, 16

Williams, D. C. (1966) *Principles of Empirical Realism*, Charles Thomas

Wittgenstein, L. (1922) *Tractatus Logico-Philosophicus*, trans. Pears, D. F. and McGuiness, B. F., Routledge 1961

Wolter, A. B. (1962) The Realism of Scotus, *Journal of Philosophy*, 59

Wolterstorff, N. (1970) *On Universals*, Chicago University Press

Index to Volume I